Finding Your Tribe

NETWORKING

A SUCCESSFUL

SMALL

BUSINESS

JOANNE DEWBERRY

First published in Great Britain in 2020

Copyright © 2020 Joanne Dewberry

The right of Joanne Dewberry to be identified as the Author has been asserted in accordance with the Copyright Design and Patents Act 1988.

ISBN 978-1-5272-6149-5 (paperback)

British Library Cataloguing in Publication Data

A CIP catalogue record for this book can be obtained from the British Library.

www.joannedewberry.co.uk

THANKS TO....

You and I wouldn't be holding this book in our hands now if it hadn't been for 3 wonderful women in my life, Syma Brown, Illana Smith and Trisha Reece, who guided me, comforted me and held my hand every step of the way. Without your clarity and unwavering support, I'd have never got past the first draft, let's face it I nearly didn't! You 3 embody what 'Networking a Successful Small Business' is all about. Thank you seems such a small word and I hope you realise how forever grateful I am.

I feel blessed to have such wonderful friends who have helped me through this process in various ways from technical support to proofreading. From everyone at Lemur Linkup, Facebook followers to the endless amounts of random tweets everyone who answered my questions, provided quotes and gave me something to think about, this book wouldn't be half as good without you!

To the Giltrow Gang - David, Charlie, Megan and Olive; I love you all very much. You remind me every day that anything is possible as long as you are prepared to go grey and lose a few marbles in the process.

Special thanks must go to my parents and brother - so Mum, Dad and David 'Special Thanks'.

> *"Some of the biggest challenges in relationships come from the fact that most people enter a relationship in order to get something: they're trying to find someone who's going to make them feel good. In reality, the only way a relationship will last is if you see your relationship as a place that you go to give, and not a place that you go to take."*
>
> *Tony Robbins*

Contents

MY STORY

Hello! My name is Joanne Dewberry - I'm the founder of small business blog www.JoanneDewberry.co.uk and co-host of Lemur Linkup Networking Group based in Poole. I live in rural Dorset, with my long-suffering partner David and our 3 wonderful children Charlie (2007), Megan (2008) and Olive (2011).

Back in 2012 I became a published author writing 'Crafting a Successful Small Business' looking at making, marketing and merchandising your craft business. At the time, I ran a party supplies business, 'Charlie Moo's', and little did I know it would take a further 8 years to publish another book. After writing a successful and interactive blog for the past 10 years whilst running numerous networking opportunities, I knew this book was inside me, I just needed the courage to let it out!

In 2010 I was named Dorset Business Mother of the Year and have numerous accolades and awards to my name. I enjoy sharing my business knowledge and expertise with other small business owners and networking provides me with a great deal of joy. Running my own business has been a way to develop new skills, meet new people and still enjoy being a full-time mother. It is hard work and I have been known to work all hours of the night as I have enjoyed a trip to the beach during the day. I am the woman hanging out her washing at 9pm. In my spare time, I like to eat and watch crime dramas sometimes at the same time!

Facebook: www.facebook.com/JoanneDewberry.co.uk
Twitter: www.twitter.com/JoanneDewberry
Instagram: www.instagram.com/JoanneDewberryUK
LinkedIn: www.linkedin.com/in/charliemoos/

AWARDS & ACHIEVEMENTS

- Highly Commended MumsClub.co.uk PR Comp 2009
- Winner of Future 100 Young Entrepreneurs 2009
- TGF Best Rated Award Winner 2009
- Langtry Manor Best Green Business Finalist 2010
- Nominated MADS Blog Award 2010 & 2011
- Winner of Dorset Business Mother of the Year 2010 – Langtry Manor
- Short listed Make Your Mark in the Market 2010
- Recognised for Very Good Service 2010
- Short listed in the World Skill Competition 2010 (Networking Mummies)
- Short listed Business Parent of the Year – Mums and Working Awards
- Enterprise Nation Ideas 101 Winner June 2010
- Short listed Best Business Mum Mumsclub Awards 2010
- Finalist Best Use of Media Mumsclub Awards 2010
- Langtry Manor Finalist in PR Initiative 2011Nominated in the Junior What's on Awards – Best Party Supplies Charlie Moo's 2011, 2012 & 2013
- Bronze Website Award Charlie Moo's Mumpreneur UK 2011
- 2011 Mumpreneur 100
- #SBS winner 26th February 2012 Theo Paphitis
- Top 20 Dorset Business Mum of the Year 2012 (Venus Awards)
- Cow Awards 2013 – Best Quirky for MerMOO Olive

- Nominated Best Online Business Venus Awards 2013
- Short listed Women in Business Women Inspiring Woman Awards 2013
- Short listed Netmums Best Party Supplier 2013
- 95 in Tots100 Chart November 2013
- Semi-Finalist Online and New Media Award Venus Awards 2014
- Short listed Parent Blogger of the Year 2014 – Mum and Working Awards
- Runner Up Best Hobby to Small Business Support for Crafting a Successful Small Business – What's on 4 Me Awards 2014
- Vuelio Top Ten Business & Finance Blog 2015
- iHubbub Best Home Blog 2016
- Short listed Parent Blogger of the Year 2016 – Mum and Working Awards
- Finalist Best Networking Group (Lemur Linkup) – Western Gazette Business Awards 2016
- Short listed Parent Blogger of the Year 2017 – Mum and Working Awards

INTRODUCTION

Fake it until you make it. Isn't that what they say? I think I have been successfully faking it since 2008. Faking it in business, faking it at the school gates, but mostly I have become adept at faking it whilst networking.

Surprisingly I am not an overly confident individual when it comes to networking in new situations. I find it difficult to walk into a room and strike up conversations with complete strangers. No, really, I do. We develop online personas, which are an awesome tool in faking it. I might ooze confidence behind my computer but in person I'm screaming 'help me!'

Online activities provide you with a vast array of statistics, insights and evidence which clearly show you, "*Hey you know what you are talking about and people like what you have to say*". In person you have to be eloquent, concise and deliver with confidence, truly believing in what you have to say. There's no room for editing and making or composing the perfect sentence. No re-dos. More importantly there is no one holding up a giant blue thumbs-up, signalling to you that you're talking sense and your comments are met with agreement. We have become a society lacking in basic communication and people-reading skills and using appropriate body language.

Most days my mornings start in chaos - as you'd expect with three children. And ultimately, they end in chaos too. My working day involves me holed up in my office at home on my own. I rarely have the need to interact or deal with people in real life situations, which in turn means I very rarely leave my comfort zone. And that, in a nutshell, is where the majority of networking issues arise from. "*I don't like networking*" is basically code for; "*I don't like leaving my comfort zone. I don't feel confident in my abilities. I don't really want to talk to people.*" I get that. I really do. We all feel like that from time to time.

So, how can you make each networking experience more positive and ultimately more rewarding? This book will guide you, step by step, through to face-to-face networking success in my jargon-free, simplistic, bitesize style, because let's face when it comes to reading a business book it often needs to be a pick up, digest and action in fleeting moments. (Usually whilst small people are swimming/football/dancing - delete as appropriate!)

Chapter One

My Networking Story

I meet a lot of parents who would love to pursue the dream of family flexible working and for the majority, this will be by running their own small business. We live in an era where it's not just those that get that light bulb moment and come up with the ultimate new product or service who get to create their own business. Sure, coming up with a great invention is fantastic, but these days, social media and technology allow us to utilise our existing skills (or learn new ones) and carve our own niche. As a result, freelancing is growing as an ever more popular alternative to full-time work.

Alongside this movement more and more types of traditional employment are offering great freelancing opportunities including corporate positions such as lawyers and solicitors. You can't ignore either the huge rise in virtual PAs (personal assistant) or VAs (virtual assistant) which is a whole massive industry in itself. There really is an opportunity available to anyone and everyone.

The majority of people I meet manage to find something that holds them back or stands in the way of them taking that full-on scary leap into self-employment. When I sat down 10 years ago and discussed a business idea with my partner, I was heavily pregnant; we already had a one-year-old and sadly very little working cash. I'd never run a business before and I wasn't even really sure what skills I would need, but what I did have was drive, determination and ultimately his support. It's been well documented that I started my first small business in 2008 selling and creating party supplies, Charlie Moo's on £56.65 (and I probably started my small business blog JoanneDewberry.co.uk on a lot less than that!). I used that money to buy a job-lot of wooden party supplies and party bag fillers to sell at summer events (whilst heavily pregnant). This provided the market research I needed to set my pricing and select my first batch of products. Once Megan was born, I used the downtime, (who am I kidding?) to learn all about building a website - mostly whilst breastfeeding. I became pretty adept at typing with one finger! There's something fierce, and in my case super-productive about a woman who's recently given birth. I've always wanted to inspire mums to see the opportunities that are out there to enable them to work from home and I soon discovered that networking provides me the perfect opportunity to do not only that, but so much more.

You cannot solely run a small business on your own, you need a support network around you and that doesn't just mean your family. Family are great but they do have a tendency to agree with you in most situations in order to make you happy. Family members will rarely challenge your thinking or make you reconsider situations and look forward: all essential steps to growing your small business. In 2009 I took my first tentative steps into networking. For me, the only way to achieve a flexible working environment that could work around my children and our family dynamics was to create one.

WHAT IS NETWORKING?

"Basically, you can't build a business on your own – so unless you happen to already know every single person you need to connect with to build your business, including all of your customers, chances are you are going to have to do some kind of networking."

Susan Payton, The Business of Stories

Traditional networking is evolving, because let's face it:

1. Networking has had a bit of a bad reputation.
2. One size most definitely doesn't fit all when it comes to networking, for me this is a key factor.

What has caused this shake up in networking circles?

As more women (and men) start-up businesses around juggling a family, traditional networking styles are no longer a good fit. 7am breakfast meetings: who are you kidding? At 7am I'm normally half asleep, arguing with Olive that a kiwi isn't a sufficient breakfast and no, it can't be followed by a chocolate bar. 7pm networking drinks: after a long day working from home, sandwiched in between school runs, swimming lessons, cooking and the occasional spot of housework, the last thing I want to do is go out in the evening and network. As parents running a business from home, we find ourselves in a catch-22 situation. We know for our business to grow we need to network, but our business and personal commitments don't always enable this to happen. With the number of small businesses in the UK at an all-time high, networking has become increasingly important.

14

We are bombarded with noise, advertising both online and off. Being able to meet people face-to-face, make genuine connections and establish relationships, (which can all then lead to referrals and recommendations), is so powerful.

Small business networking comes in so many varieties now; from traditional meetings, relaxed lunches, co-working spaces, trade conferences and of course online. This means you can adapt and tailor networking to suit your needs, the needs of your clients and/or your weekly schedule.

I think I've always been one of life's networkers – probably without thinking about it. I think it stems from my love of talking. I'm very gifted in the conversation department, but I'm also a good listener and can usually see cross promotions/collaborations others may miss. I also really like helping people, enabling them to move forward, to work with others and such. I love the buzz I get from seeing my suggestion/idea come into its own. I clearly see the value in making real-life business connections and friends. This is a key factor in networking. Mums in business account for one in seven of all self-employed people in the UK. The largest numbers can be found working as highly skilled freelancers, particularly in two areas: associate professional and technical occupations (137,000) and professional occupations (125,000). The third-largest group (123,000) work in caring, leisure and other service occupations. (Information from: The Association of Independent Professionals and Self Employed (ISPE) report, 'Exploring the rise of self-employment in the modern economy' 2008.) I believe mums in business are breeding a new kind of networking group, flexible but also more nurturing, as is our nature.

Networking Mummies 2009-2011

(Rebranded The Families Network LTD as of 2018)

When I started Charlie Moo's, back in 2008, after the initial start-up phase, organising stock, prices and building a website, it soon became obvious to me that not only did I want to talk to other small business owners like me, I also wanted/needed to learn things too. However, by early 2009, about six months in, I knew I needed help. Help to grow this new business in a number of areas; building a customer base, marketing, everyday things like social media advice, (this is back in the day before Instagram and Pinterest), HMRC and basically someone to talk through the million ideas running through my mind. I needed to meet people in a similar situation to myself. I needed to find retail outlets/craft fairs but also to progress my learning around websites and ecommerce. I literally knew nothing and although Google and YouTube were my new BFFs, I missed people. To start with I joined online small business forums – safe havens within which to chat with small business owners across the UK back when Facebook didn't dominate our lives or businesses. My first dalliance with networking came after a few online chats with another small business owner and mother, Laura Morris. We were fuelled by the fact we both wanted to network locally (she lived in the next village) but both of us were full-time carers to our young children. We decided to meet at our local toddler group, somewhere I went weekly and thus felt safe. We soon discovered we shared a realisation that there must be other parents building small businesses with children like us. There wasn't anything tailored to our situation as parents with children under five (who therefore weren't at school). We couldn't go to 7am breakfasts and we didn't have the energy at 7pm to nip out to network (I still don't have the energy now!). We needed somewhere we could bring the children. Together we formulated a plan to organise one informal networking event for mums in business and see what happened. The idea was simple and we never set out to make this into a business. We literally intended for mums to be able to meet with or without their children, with other like-minded mums running businesses from home. We posted an open invitation on our local Netmums site with details about our first meeting which we held unofficially at a soft play centre. Eight mums with businesses and their children turned up for that first meeting in February 2009 and neither Laura nor I were prepared for the whirlwind which became Networking Mummies. Before long we had a basic website set up, a full schedule of coffee mornings, evening speaker events and discounted entry at soft play - something to suit everyone.

Running a networking group is actually a lot of fun (albeit hard work). You get to meet an enormous amount of people from a vast array of businesses. You also get an insight into how people interact with each other and which networking techniques work and ultimately which don't. We held an exhibition in October 2009 as part of the Mums in Business Week showcasing local small businesses, services and products plus the opportunity to network. During the exhibition Laura and I were approached by a couple of ladies who wanted to replicate what we were doing in Hampshire, under the Networking Mummies umbrella. We soon realised other people shared our vision for making real-life connections with other small businesses whilst raising a family. This led us to provide Networking Mummies franchising opportunities throughout the UK.

In 2011, after a difficult pregnancy with our third child, Olive, I decided to sell my half of Networking Mummies and concentrate on writing my first book, Crafting a Successful Small Business, because crazily my three most productive years ever have been those that followed the birth of a child. I'd never stopped networking online and have always taken an active role in networking but sometimes you just need that face-to-face banter. Being part of Networking Mummies had given me the confidence to talk about my business in front of other professionals. For a long time, I saw myself as a full-time mum, end of. Now I know that's simply not true, that I'm an entrepreneur no different to Duncan Bannatyne. I just work around my children.

Notable Information:

Co-Founder: 2009-2011

Awards: Shortlisted in the World Skill Competition 2010

Franchises: Five

Lemur Linkup 2014-Present

I started meeting up with local blogger and mummy-to-six Kara Guppy (www.Chelseamamma.com) as our children are a similar age, after meeting at a blogging event. Our youngest daughters soon became friends making it easy to meet up to chat about all things blogging whilst the children played. In 2014, Kara, alongside soft play owner Jackie Richmond and PR manager Emma Collins, were looking to start a child-friendly networking group using Lemur Landings as the base. Given my involvement with Networking Mummies I was invited to join the team. At this time Olive was three and I'd really missed networking with other small businesses owners with children so of course I jumped at the chance to be involved.

As Lemur Linkup is co-hosted by Jackie, who owns the soft play centre, we are able to offer discounted rates for those bringing children and free to those who don't. You would be surprised how many small business owners come on a monthly basis without children. I think small businesses prefer a low-cost pay-as-you-go option to networking as this gives them flexibility and freedom. Unlike Networking Mummies this is not a registered business, but a sideline for Lemur Landings making it far less stressful for me and the other co-hosts.

Our children are able to run around whilst we can network; our meetings are monthly on a Monday, which is a great way to kick-start the week. They are term time only meaning we don't formally meet in August or December and dates are dictated by half terms, inset days, etc. Each meeting has a business theme and guest speaker. The networking group fulfils my networking needs by providing me with a support framework/tribe. What I get from the group business-wise and developmentally makes it well worth attending, even if at times it is a little noisy! As we hit our 6th year, circumstances change, children grow up, small businesses develop, Lemur Linkup is currently co-hosted by myself and Jackie and we very rarely have any small children attending.

> *'I had no expectations of friendship when I started Lemur Linkup but it's such a good feeling to have you as a friend, along with others from the group.'*
>
> *Jackie Richmond, Lemur Landings*

Notable Information:

Co-host: 2014-Present

Awards: Finalist in Networking Group Category – Western Gazette Business Awards 2016

One of the many reasons I enjoy networking personally is the opportunity to be completely independent of all my other endless responsibilities. Once you become a parent you easily adopt the title of being someone's mum (or dad), known basically to others by whom your child/children are, which is probably even worse if your child is one of those undesirable types, which I fear a couple of mine may be! At networking events, rather than being known as or referred to as "Olive's mummy", I'm Joanne; I'm treated as a professional, regarded for my business and blogging knowledge and not chatting about the latest school craze or known purely for my tardiness and excellent use of sushi ginger for Harvest Festival (true story). Lemur Linkup is mainly attended by mothers of some sort, whilst some have little children or school-aged children, others have grown up ones but being a parent and running a business are a common theme amongst attendees. This common thread can make conversations a lot easier to start. There is a lovely balance between being a mum and being a business owner although it's flipping hard work (not gonna lie!). IPSE issued a report that shows there has been a significant rise in the number of self-employed working mothers. The figure reached 594,000 in 2017, which is 14% of the overall UK solo self-employed population. 'The total number of mothers working in highly skilled freelance occupations has almost doubled since 2008, amounting to an increase of 96%. Since 2016, the proportion of the total number of highly skilled freelancers who are working mothers has also risen by 10%.' This provides evidence that parents (in particular mothers) want more flexibility in their work life and careers as well as being near to and hands on with their children, which ultimately freelancing/self-employed careers provide an abundance of.

Chapter Two

Why Does My Business Need To Network?

According to the Oxford English dictionary, the definition of networking is *"exchanging information and forming professional connections through social meetings"* – the emphasis being on social. In order to get social, you really need to leave your house, because remember the magic happens outside your comfort zone.

Michael Tobin's book Live, Love, Work, Prosper (2018) states there are 3 million home-based businesses in the UK contributing £300 billion to the UK economy, meaning that a lot of the time communication is undertaken digitally. Some days, I don't speak to anyone until I collect the children from school and my son is a 12-year-old with a somewhat limited after school vocabulary. Not only can this make working from home a really lonely experience but it's easy to actually start to forget how to communicate with real life people.

Networking has sadly amassed a bit of a bad reputation, think suits and awkward conversations in a room full of people trying to sell at you. I can see why people tend to avoid it. However, the correct type of networking is not only vital but also an inexpensive tool for your small business. For me the emphasis on networking is always around the idea of developing a tribe, building a support team around you

24

who will ultimately help you grow your business far better than looking for a quick-fix sale. Transactional relationships can be counterproductive - attending events where the end strategies or sole intent of people there is to sell to you will always leave you feeling disappointed. Remember it's 'networking' not 'sales meeting'. Networking is a long game, it can take a while to reap the fruits of your labours, but at the same time it should be fun.

When I first started Charlie Moo's back in 2008, I felt intimidated by other small businesses, I felt too inexperienced to go to networking events; that I personally didn't have anything of value to offer to other small business owners. At the time my children Charlie and Megan were both under three so many events locally just didn't work logistically for me or my situation. Breakfast meetings were an impossibility, and as for events after 7pm, quite frankly, I was too tired to go out and make small talk. Realising that I wasn't the only mum in business with a young family feeling and thinking like this was in fact a revelation, I'd go as far as to say it has been a catalyst for most of what has happened in my small business since.

Through networking, I developed a vital support network for my business – one that I regularly consult with when I need advice, support, training or a real person to rant at (who isn't my partner as this can be no good for your home life). And vice versa, my network knows that I'm there for them. I've really gotten to know people and when this happens you develop strong bonds with other small businesses. The lines naturally blur, some of my best friends who I see socially, are those I have met through networking. It's simple really, once you like and ultimately trust a small business owner this will inevitably and sometimes quickly blossom into friendship. Networking where you build yourself a support network/tribe provides you with a means in which to develop important skills both socially and small business related. You can share knowledge and experiences, plus being around others also helps to reduce stress and anxiety.

As the old saying goes, "*It's not WHAT you know, but WHO*", and I believe this is really important in small business. If you don't network, then you don't build and develop a community around you and therefore, you never meet those people worth knowing. Your first-generation contacts may never actually buy from you or even need your services/products, but they will almost certainly know or meet someone else who does. Instead, think of your first generation of contacts as your shopfront - leading the way for others to come in and purchase services or goods.

Having a support network of people to talk through ideas and problems with is essential to my day-to-day routine, and knowing that these people are there when you need them can help to alleviate the loneliness of running a small business on your own. Happy, stress-free individuals are conducive to a successful small business.

WHY DO I NEED TO NETWORK?

Sometimes analogies are the best way to describe things so here goes. You wouldn't plant a carrot seed and expect to eat that carrot today. It takes time; you need to nourish, nurture and wait patiently for that carrot to grow. In the same way you wouldn't expect to meet someone for the first time and instantly become the best of friends (however that's not to say that can't happen!) you need to build a level of trust, mutual respect and get to know someone before you will want to start working with them. In terms of our carrot analogy, networking events are your gardening time. You are putting in the time to nourish/nurture relationships on a face-to-face level.

The possibilities through networking are endless from reaching new customers, creating conversations, researching opportunities, to increasing word-of-mouth promotion. As well as developing skills, networking allows you to access a range of knowledge, expertise and be around industry influencers (particularly true of genre specific or trade show events). The wider your network becomes, the more responsive your small business is, especially if you build a network that benefits your customers/clients. The best approach to networking is cultivating connections you already have.

5 Reasons to Network

Networking raises your small business profile: Raising your profile helps you to become a go-to person in your genre. A go-to person can be a powerful resource to those within your network, the person they turn to for advice, support and will immediately think of you in any situation. A 'go-to person' gets to really know the people within the network and can make valuable connections.

'Try not to become a man of success. Rather become a man of value.'

Albert Einstein

Cost effective form of advertising: You aren't just networking with those attending the group on the day, (previously referred to as your 'first generation contacts'), you are networking with a wider audience i.e. your second and third generation contacts. These are the connections of each person at the event, the people they talk to and socialise with – the people who could potentially be customers of yours. So, remember, you are never just networking the room, which is why it's important to get to know people rather than small businesses.

Physical engagement increases your online interaction: People will make more time to connect with you online, to continue conversations, to see where collaborations might occur and develop ideas they may already have after they've met you in person, (well, if they like you!). I also find that social media enables me to keep up to date with an individual's small business news so that when you do see them at a networking event you have a list of things to start conversations about.

85% of all jobs are filled via networking: Years ago, while working in childcare, I met a lady during a training session who owned a day nursery and she told me her current deputy was about to leave. We sat next to each other for a few sessions and got chatting, made a connection, had a chuckle, did some group work together and had similar opinions and creative ideas. A few weeks later I was shocked to get a phone call from her at my place of work asking me to come for an interview. I guess you could say I was "headhunted" but the facts are simple, we made a connection, which in turn, made her think we could work together. This connection that might not have come across in a formal interview setting. Networking fills job vacancies whether that be through finding the ideal candidate at a networking event or chatting with someone who knows someone who would be ideal.

Group therapy: I can literally go days without real human interaction, which is common especially for mums in business, freelancers and solopreneurs working from home. Through networking you soon recognise the importance of celebrating your successes, wins, milestones and achievements. When you build a support network around you, they too will celebrate these wins for you - motivating you to strive even further. Our networking allies become our cheer squad rejoicing in the wins and motivating in the lows.

NETWORKING IS A SKILL

It's a skill which can be improved. The more you network, the more people you meet, the better you will get at networking and the less it will feel like a chore and more a vital cog in your small business. Networking uses skills we lose from conducting interactions online, such as reading body language, active listening and talking. Networking is long-term, and good relationships will always outperform good deals - which are usually short term. Networking opens doors to new opportunities that aren't available or even on your radar unless your leave your comfort zone, in my case home office. Networking really is all about being in the right place at the right time consistently. I love this story from Amanda Davey, (Tilia Publishing UK), which really does go to show the power of networking once you stop thinking about how to sell your business to others but instead focus on what you can do for them:

"*My grandfather was the civil engineer appointed to the Aberfan Tribunal to investigate the causes of the terrible disaster in 1966. The day of his appointment he was at a TA dinner (he'd been involved since WWI) and the CO offered his support if anything was needed. The following day the Imperial College investigators said they really needed special vehicles to get across all the loose spoil. My grandfather said he knew someone who might have an answer and rang the CO. Turned out the Canadians had loaned two tank-like trucks for testing that they'd not found a use for yet, so they were able to use those. I use this to explain how I see the power of networking. It's not about how many business cards you can get rid of at an event it's about how many times you can have the 'Ah ha, I might have just the answer' moment and really make a difference."* Amanda Davey, Tilia Publishing UK

Once you look further into building and extending the network of people around you, rather than selling products/services, your small business will progress and grow far more effectively. What might seem like common sense or easy for you, may be confusing or difficult for other small business owners. By providing value to your networking connections you make yourself an expert and an indispensable asset in someone else's business.

SHOULD YOU HAVE AN OBJECTIVE WHEN ATTENDING NETWORKING EVENTS?

Sometimes we can over analyse things, isn't just meeting new people enough? A report, 'Exploring the rise of self-employment in the modern economy' by Kingston University and IPSE (March 2018), provides statistics that show more mothers than ever before are choosing to work for themselves, putting the current figure at 594,000. This means the number of freelance mothers has actually doubled since 2008. One in seven self-employed people in the UK is a mother. Freelancers spend 95% of their time on their own. Getting out and meeting new people not only opens up a whole host of opportunities and possible collaborations but also provides you with real life people to talk to, and this simple interaction shouldn't be underestimated.

"*The thought of selling myself is what puts me off going to networking events*" and this is where many small businesses go wrong. Networking isn't really about selling yourself. In fact, it's much more about developing relationships and making connections within your local business community. These connections will enable you to grow and develop your small business, either through collaborations, referrals or through learning and skill-based opportunity.

> *"One person, one conversation and one relationship at a time."*
>
> *Jill Celeste, 2017*

This idea can really help with that feeling of overwhelm when you enter a room full of people. Choose one person, get to know their business really well, follow up from the office and reap the benefits of a blossoming relationship.

Seeking advice from others is paramount. There will also be someone who has been or is where you are on your small business journey; who can offer support, guidance and advice; who enables you to build your support network/tribe and most of the time this isn't actually with potential customers but with collaborators. This then allows you to then connect with an even more diverse range of contacts.

Chapter Seven looks more closely at defining and setting actionable networking goals.

WELLBEING, HAPPINESS AND HEALTH

Networking for me has been extremely beneficial to developing my own self-esteem and identity. Face to face networking plays an important role in offsetting the sense of isolation that many small business owners feel, the isolation which in turn can affect our mood. Networking events can be the sole contributing factor that encourages homeworkers and freelancers to actually leave their home office and get out of the house. Not only does networking provide a break from work, which we all know is a great productivity increaser (there's nothing worse or more demotivating than staring blankly at a screen, frozen and unable to write/produce anything - I should know, this book has been a labour of love over 4 long, long years!). But more importantly, networking is an opportunity to interact with real-life, walking, talking human people! Engaging in physical interaction such as talking face-to-face instead of via email, having a group discussion with your peers, somewhere to vent, tackle issues or even simply having a coffee and a chat can make all the difference. As we start to more consciously value our mental wellbeing and recognise just how lonely life can be for a homeworker, more networking groups are evolving to tackle these issues. Burnout, stress and self-sabotaging are common place among entrepreneurs, but having an array of like-minded people to bounce ideas off, collaborate, check a piece of work is enormously reassuring – providing home workers with the opportunity to look after their mental wellbeing and network with like-minded individuals.

"Happiness leads to greater profits"

Shawn Achor

Our own personal happiness should be a core ethos in everything we do but it seldom is. It probably doesn't surprise you that happy people are more productive, creative, better at problem-solving and more effective decision makers. Being around other like-minded people and doing fun things that make us happy are clearly good for us, but how can networking make us happy?

Positive vibes; Your vibe attracts Your tribe. This isn't just an Instagram hashtag, it's real life. I'm really grateful for the people in my tribe/support network and I can hand on heart say that not one of them is toxic as quite frankly I don't have time for that! It's a common myth that success makes you happy; however, it is actually the other way around. Being happy brings more enjoyment and successes into your life.

You may think that happiness and success go hand-in-hand because success causes happiness, but it's not true. Happy people not only work better they make you feel better and happier yourself. Have you noticed that before? When you spend time with someone who makes you feel happy, positive and enthused, you want to repeat that transaction again and again. Why is that? Because the positive feelings you generate by being friendly to one person extend beyond the actual interaction. According to a study by Nicholas Christakis, Ph. D in the British Medical Journal.

"The good feelings generated by your friendly interactions create a happiness ripple that travels as far as three connections away. This is due to the secretion of oxytocin. Oxytocin is the neurochemical that has allowed us to become social creatures. It enables us to feel empathy, which in turn helps us feel close and bonded to others when it's released. People are vital to our emotional, intellectual, and physical wellbeing. This is true whether these people are family members, our everyday friends and confidantes, our small business contacts, or merely the people with whom we have a nodding acquaintance with."

A study from the National Bureau of Economic Research polled 5,000 people (DeNucci 2014) and discovered the number of real-life friends you have positively correlates with your wellbeing, more so than income, demographics, and personality. Money can't make you happy as doubling your number of friends has a similar effect on your wellbeing as doubling your income. We can look here at Dunbar's number (Dr Robin Dunbar 1990) the cognitive limit to the number of people one knows and is able to keep social contact with maintaining stable social relationships; relationships in which an individual knows who each person is and how each person relates to every other person. There is no real value citied to the actual number but it's commonly thought to be 150. In terms of networking you meet 150 people who know 150 people meaning you are only ever two handshakes away from 20,000 people.

"One conclusion is blatantly clear from my happiness research: everyone from contemporary scientists to ancient philosophers agrees that having strong social bonds is probably the most meaningful contributor to happiness."

Gretchen Rubin's The Happiness Project

4 BENEFITS TO BEING HAPPY

1. **Improved health**: This leads to fewer sick days. When you are self-employed, sick days are usually a luxury we can ill afford (pun intended!). Who knew just being happy has so many health benefits? For example, happier people eat more fruit and vegetables, exercise regularly and sleep better; being happier leads to healthier lifestyle choices.

2. **Develop resilience**: Resilience looks at the ability to bounce back from setbacks and overcome them. We humans are set on a negative default which makes it incredibly easy to get caught up on what went wrong, how we failed and letting these feelings bring us down. Resilience enables us to instead work things out encouraging us to turn failures into learning experiences and making a win from a setback. Being happy, means you feel less conflict and negativity making you more willing to look for win-win outcomes from even bad situations.

3. **Better quality relationships**: These are relationships both at work and socially.

4. **Better Performance**: Increased mental wellbeing leads to better performance, increased productivity and sales. This factor to me seems key in making sure we are happy. (Maybe if I'd been happier it wouldn't have taken me so long to write a second book! Joking, I'm a black belt in procrastination!).

There are many health benefits to being happy, these are just a few. When networking provides so many opportunities to develop resilience, build better quality relationships and increase productivity, increasing our overall well-being and happiness it seems counterproductive that face to face networking is so far down on our list of small business priorities.

Walking based networking groups are growing in popularity and it's easy to see why. Walking is good exercise plus as it's low impact it's accessible to everyone regardless of their fitness levels. Walking boosts stress-easing endorphins, reduces fatigue and increases circulation, all in turn improving your heart's health. After walking for even an hour my whole mental outlook is different, it's true that fresh air certainly does blow the cobwebs away. I organise a monthly walk where I meet up with other small business owners. We walk fast enough to still be able to talk properly but still walk with a purpose rather than ambling. This increases your energy levels, metabolism, self-esteem and ultimately improves your mood which makes you happy at the same time as developing valuable working relationships. We talk about all those things you normally would in our networking environment. Being outdoors has restorative properties, such as increasing your short-term memory and reducing stress. In Japan 'shinrin-yoku' or forest-bathing has become a cornerstone of preventive health care and healing in Japanese medicine since its development in the 1980s.

Forest Bathing

I happened upon the idea whilst researching the benefits of walking and being outside whilst developing the theory behind 'Netwalking Sessions'.

Guided Forest Bathing comprises of guidelines which take you on a gentle walk through the forest whilst stopping to offer 'invitations'. These invitations are to activities that are designed to heighten our sensory awareness. The first invitation was to close our eyes and use our other senses 'Concentric Listening'. The idea is to expand your awareness whilst engaging your auditory sense with the nature around you. We stood still, listening carefully to everything immediately around us. After a few moments the Guide invited us to change the direction we were standing (using north, south, east, west, however I've no idea if I was stood in the correct direction but this is far from the actual point of it). When you turn off one of your senses, in this case sight, it's always surprising how much your others pipe up. The heat from the sun on certain parts of your face and arms, the feel of the tall grass around your calves, the smell of the meadow, the rustling leaves, an aeroplane flying past and the feel of the spongy moss under your feet. All things I usually take for granted or dismiss as my mind is somewhere else. This invitation has an incredible way of making you feel calm and relaxed. You automatically notice that your mind stops racing and your breathing changes from natural to long deep breaths savouring every moment and completely filling your lungs with air. Forest Bathing changes your perspective on the world around you providing both a sense of peace and balance.

WAYS TO INCORPORATE FOREST BATHING AT HOME

Forest Bathing invitations are devised to develop a meaningful relationship with nature, enhance your mood and clear your mind. We spend so much of our time connected to phones, computers, rushing from school to gymnastics, Scouts and at some point, eating and sleeping (and that's just my Monday!), it's not surprising we burn out. Adding some kind of Forest Bathing activities into our weekly routine is a great way to calm down, feel at one with nature, absorb the positive energy of trees and cleanse from the inside out.

Here are two of the invitations I took part in during our Guided Forest Bathing session which self-employed home workers could easily adopt into their busy day with maximum wellness impact. The 'Sit Spot' and 'Wandering' you could even add onto the end or beginning of a Netwalking session with small business friends. I think there is a great power in bringing networking and the outdoors together. All you need is a natural place (beach, forest, meadow) or even in your garden and ideally aim to spend 20 minutes on either invitation.

Sit Spot

The perfect invitation for your garden, especially if like ours it is a wildlife friendly one, you are surrounded by a diverse ecosystem. Practice spending time there just sitting fully engaged with what is going on around you. Make this your daily relaxation time whereby you can leave the hustle and bustle of life behind. No phones, no paper or pens, no people, just 20 minutes to relax and absorb the tranquillity and calmness around you. If you visit daily or weekly you will start to notice more the changing seasons, new sights and sounds, your feelings and the connections you feel with nature. Since our Forest Bathing visit, I have started to add a sit spot into my daily routine normally over my morning coffee.

Wandering

This is one of the simplest Forest Bathing invitations. All you need to do is find a trail, in a forest or natural area which you can easily get to from your home. Personally, I think somewhere accessible by foot would be perfect. If you have to get in a car to go there it will begin to feel like a chore/time drain, therefore, the likelihood of you keeping this up long term is limited. Choose a route about a mile long with a diverse ecosystem with different types of environment (meadows, woodland, water) and that the area is quiet.

Let your instincts take over with absolutely no agenda other than to be fully present in that moment, start walking. Practice a quiet presence, open all your senses; touch, smell and sound, whilst mindfully moving through the landscape. Remember physical exercise is not the primary goal, you aren't looking to increase your heart rate so don't rush. The main aim is to make Forest Bathing a regular activity enabling you to develop a meaningful relationship with nature, clear your mind and relax.

Lemur Linkup has been running now for five years and I've already developed strong personal and business bonds as have many other members. For 2018, I wanted to do something different to foster not only networking relationships but ease the boredom and loneliness that comes from working from home, which in turn can have a detrimental effect on your wellbeing. On a whim, I started monthly Self-employed Team Building Socials (I really need a better name) introducing activities that not only get individuals out of the house, in the fresh air and exercise but also craft-based sessions too where everyone can relax and get lost in creativity.

> *'I've attended the archery and rifle shooting days so far and I've had a ball! I feel like it's really cementing the relationships I've made through networking and it's fantastic to try new things and boost my confidence too. I'm really appreciating a couple of hours out of the office to allow some fresh perspective on my business.'*
>
> *Alexia Browning, Made By Me Craft Parties.*

We will look more at these events in Chapter 3 but they are relevant here in terms of happiness and wellbeing.

Chapter Three

How To Find Networking Events

Now we are all clued up and understand the benefits of networking to both our self, wellbeing, happiness and of course our small business. You might be thinking about giving this face to face local networking a chance. But where is the best place to start? Research. There are a plethora of business support and networking groups out there, and the way that each operates varies dramatically. Some charge a subscription fee and require you to perform X, Y and Z in order to remain a member, others are more relaxed, informal operating on a pay-as-you-go basis, with no real expectations from you as a user. Some are organised on a voluntary basis, meeting in coffee shops which reduces the need for paid attendance instead concentrating on the goal of simply getting business owners together.

I believe you have to visit a variety of face-to-face networking groups a couple of times to know which you prefer and works best for you. Social media is, as always, a great starting point, I sometimes wonder how we did anything without. By now you probably have a Facebook page, Twitter account and have maybe joined community-based business groups on Facebook. Use these already established connections to seek out and source appropriate networking events. Sometimes the simplest option is the easiest: literally just ask other local businesses, especially those within your industry, where they

44

network; can you go along with them as a guest? Going with someone you already know can make things less daunting. Consider utilising local hashtag hours on Twitter (#DorsetHour, for example is used on a Monday evening 7:30pm-8:30pm) there are likely to be networking groups advertising their upcoming events during this hour and a plethora of local businesses to ask all in one place at the same time.

Websites like www.FindNetworkingEvents.com and Eventbrite should be your next port of call too. FindNetworkingEvents.com is a great website which lists events by region, town/city, whether they are aimed at women only, business shows or workshops and seminars, the only downside is this platform requires the event organiser to list them so it's not an exhaustive list. Eventbrite allows you to search for events in your area and a popular platform for those events that require you to sign up or pay beforehand. This too isn't an exhaustive list.

MAKING A LIST OF PROS AND CONS

Finding the events is easy, deciding which to attend is harder. When looking for networking opportunities and events make yourself a list of pros and cons, detailing each aspect of the event including expenses, expectations, consistency etc.

EXPENSE

Does this networking group charge an upfront annual fee? If they do, does this suit your needs? For me as a working mum life can be so unpredictable and uncertain no matter how much you plan (I've literally had to miss two different networking events this week alone due to a poorly child). I personally wouldn't want sick children and the never-ending school holidays to mean I paid a fortune to be part of a network that I can never attend. However, you can see the subscription fee as a perk of the group. Some people may argue that paying a yearly subscription means you have invested in your networking, committing to taking the time to go every month and are therefore more likely to interact and grow your network. Paying a subscription acts as an instigation and encouragement to actually attend meetings that you might choose to opt out of last minute if you hadn't paid. From my research those who have paid networking subscriptions believe that everyone there takes networking more seriously than free events and are there to get leads and to meet other small businesses owners who can help on progress through their own business journey.

Anne Cornish VA pays a yearly subscription to Athena Network, who have branches up and down the UK for women in business. She believes those that choose a subscription are *"more committed to attend their regular meetings as they want to get some ROI[1] back, will have a strategy in place for each meeting, and are more likely to*

---

[1] ROI - Return on Investment and in this case that's financial.

collaborate and give referrals as they get to know their fellow networking members better".

Make sure you also consider what do you actually get for your annual subscription fee. Some of the larger UK business support networks offer perks like legal protection and financial health checks. This is a personal choice and has to be judged by listing the pros and cons for making a large financial outlay on networking. Make sure the scheme is actually worth joining for you. If you pay up to get the freebies but never use the networking group and events or haven't made any lasting connections, developed your support network/tribe then was this money really well spent? Each group will vary considerably, which means it's vital to thoroughly research groups, remember you are investing in a minimum of a year's membership. Take the Athena Network for example; paid subscription members get a half-day masterclass on networking strategy (a course that is elsewhere priced between £250-£350) the purpose of which is to enable them to make the most of their networking, by planning their networking strategy in alignment with their business strategy. Each monthly meeting comprises two delivered training sessions which are both based around developing skills (specifically networking and business skills). There is also support and encouragement to develop public speaking experience which aids the members, both in their business and personal development. Each of the Athena Network groups have a one discipline representation, i.e. only one photographer, one virtual assistant; however, across most regions there will be ample opportunities provided to increase networking and collaborations through informal free coffee mornings and larger seasonal social events. Athena Network has around 150 groups up and down the UK which are open to all members regardless of location. Like most networking groups Athena Network also runs a private national members only closed Facebook group providing a safe haven to promote your small business, request advice, support others and get referrals. Natalia DaCosta, Athena Network Bournemouth, says,

"We have seen local and international connections being made in this way [via the Facebook group]. And it is a brilliant way for our members to source their suppliers – I have seen a specialist "green" events company that have managed to source 80% of their suppliers just through the Athena Network."

Natalia DaCosta also provided other evidence supporting small business growth and development achieved through the Athena Network group with members achieving national media coverage as well as writing and publishing books via the relationships and collaborations forged through networking. Athena Network HQ also hosts regular online training and networking sessions moving the emphasis from local networking to national, providing even wider opportunities for networking and collaborations.

> *"The Athena Network, does not pretend to be for everyone, but it is most definitely for those women who are looking to invest [time and money] in their business and in themselves."*
>
> *Natalia DaCosta.*

Do You Want to be Able to Dip In and Out?

> *"I want flexibility, not an event that I HAVE to attend every week/month at the same time. I'd also rather pay less for membership and more for the events, so I'm in control of being able to choose the events that I believe will give me better ROI."*
>
> *Jo Lee Personal Coach, Life Atlas Coaching.*

I prefer not to pay a subscription but instead develop relationships more naturally and organically rather than being forced to as you are part of the same group. I like informal groups whereby I can attend when it suits my needs. Most informal pay-as-you-go groups run in two ways. You pay upfront for a ticket meaning you can go when you like or they are free to attend but you'd be expected to buy a drink at the venue. Local Chambers of Commerce offer discount rates to chamber members but still allow outsiders to come but charge a little more. I also like workshops and seminars where there is opportunity to learn something new alongside meeting other like-minded businesses in the area. The learning opportunities provide value to the networking events.

Lemur Linkup is specifically designed with parents running a small business in mind from our soft play venue to our schedule, we don't meet formally in August (summer holidays) or December – the busiest times for parents. It also is a free non-profit group (you only pay for drinks or a discounted soft play rate if you are bringing children) therefore if anything unexpected crops up, sick children, a short deadline, car broke down, etc. you aren't stressed about missing the event or the spent money.

"I'm less inclined to join in if the price is higher as self-employed, I need to earn not spend."

Jo Stratton, Jo's Healing Cabin.

The great thing is there are so many free networking groups about where the organiser's primary aim is to get local small business owners together. Poole Business Owners Community states "the aim of this group is to provide business owners with the opportunity to meet other business owners in a friendly, relaxed and informal setting."

DOES THE NETWORKING GROUP HAVE SPECIFIC REQUIREMENTS?

Subscription-based networking groups usually have some kind of specific requirements that businesses are expected to fulfil in order to join this network.

For example, do you need to make regular referrals? Now, if I had to bring something (referrals/journalists/new clients) to the networking table every meeting I think after a while I would find this very stressful. I do this because I want to, there are no expectations from either party. For me, networking should be relaxing and more importantly fun and endorphin boosting, not an ugly business chore.

Finding out about requirements to join a group is really important. Do you need to commit to attending a certain number of times? Are you required to bring a friend along? Can you attend or is your genre already represented? Some groups only allow one person from each business genre.

How Often Do They Meet and What Time?

I currently go to four different monthly events, meaning I'm out of the office once a week, some networking groups meet weekly or fortnightly. I like monthly, as it's regular, but there is enough time in between events for something to happen. Actual time will vary greatly, there are still lots of networking groups that meet in the morning for breakfast, either before the working day starts 7am, or 9am as your day begins, evening events and some networking groups even meet at weekends. There is something to suit everyone. I personally like to network straight from dropping the children off from school 9/10-12 works well for me as I still have a few hours to work before I collect the children from school. Morning networking events are less disruptive to your day than midday lunches and far more work-oriented than evenings which usually are in pubs/bars with the option of alcohol available.

How Far Away Are They?

How much of your working day do you want to be out of the office? Are you happy to write a whole day off? I usually attend networking events that happen at 10am as this means I have an hour to get there from school drop off and I know I'll usually be home by 1 giving me two hours before school pick up. I tend not to travel more than 40 minutes/one hour away, I ALWAYS have something to do if I turn up early, ie. check my emails, write notes, edit posts, etc. I like to utilise my travel time.

CAN I ACTUALLY ATTEND?

Some subscription-based groups pride themselves on only allowing one member from each genre, to eliminate competition. Trade2Business for example have this as a selling point, they have an annual membership of £100 which guarantees no competition alongside a £40 a month meeting fee. Visitors can attend as many times as they wish as long as their business doesn't conflict with an existing member. Which reminded me of Amanda Davey's, comment (Tilia Publishing UK): "*So many of the paid subscription organisations demand referrals, which to me is the antithesis*[2] *of relationship building*".

In some ways this is a good idea as nobody really wants to network with a roomful of just photographers say. But it can also reduce the pool of people at these events, because let's face it we all have different skills, strengths, weaknesses and personalities regardless of our business genre. Later in this chapter I'll look more at what kinds of networking groups there are and how useful same genre networking groups can be for you and your business. However, that's

---

[2] Antithesis = direct opposite

not to say there aren't merits in one person only, I think here this is a personal choice and you need to consider who you want to network with and why. There is no wrong or right answer just what you are more comfortable with. Many of these subscription-based networking groups will have some kind of guest options and/or taster sessions, try lots of networking groups/events out to really get a feel for the group and the people through regular attendance.

IS THERE ONLINE SUPPORT?

Long gone are the days of forums; everything is on Facebook now and you will find most networking groups have some kind of online support too. For Lemur Linkup we have a closed Facebook group, this enables people to connect before and after the events, seek advice, help others and keep conversations going. If a group is closed on Facebook you will have to request to join and anything you write is private in the group. Some groups will be public which means any comments you make will be visible to everyone. Online groups enhance your networking experience no end and usually mean no matter what time of the day or even weekends there is always someone around to help/respond to you. Private online groups add value to events from both the organisers and attendees' point of view, for example we recently discussed Facebook Lives; our private group gives people a non-judgemental place to trial new skills and ask for critiques and feedback in a safe environment.

WHAT IS THE FORMAT?

Lemur Linkup meets monthly, always on a Monday mid-month (school holidays having a bearing on the specific date), and we have an hour dedicated to a speaker. These are often members of the group who get to run sessions in the area they specialise enabling them to teach others new techniques and enhance their status as an expert in their genre. This is also a great way to learn more about someone's small business and again strengthen connections. I also actively seek out speakers for specific topics that may have arisen during other meetings. "I definitely prefer events that have a speaker as that helps to act as an icebreaker." Illana Smith, Hari Hari Curry. You will find a large number or groups use the networking, speaker, networking sandwich approach to meetings.

WHO ARE YOU LOOKING TO MEET?

Sometimes the right networking group will be determined by who you are looking to connect with. CEO's are more likely to hang out at local chamber events whereas your SME (small/medium enterprise) is more likely to be at morning events/breakfast meetings. If your ideal client/customer or collaborator isn't attending the same events as you, then mix it up a bit and alter the networking groups you attend slightly.

THINK OUTSIDE THE BOX

Networking opportunities don't have to be traditionally or formally organised events to offer opportunities to collaborate and develop relationships. For example, there are plenty of co-working spaces that not only provide excellent alternative working environments (and we all know how productive we are once we leave our home offices), but they are also a great place to meet other small businesses owners. Small business training, workshops and courses are another "kill two birds with one stone" opportunity you get to update your training, learn new skills, etc. and there are always opportunities to meet and chat with those around you finding out more about their business. The good thing about training is that you meet people you wouldn't normally, not only making you test your social skills but widening your network even more. Do something that makes you comfortable; when you're relaxed and happy this is when conversation will easily flow and relationships will develop. There are a variety of other networking opportunities.

OTHER NETWORKING OPPORTUNITIES

"Surround yourself with like-minded people. Success is a group activity."

Angel Alzona

Continuing on from 'thinking outside of the box', networking opportunities do not have to be organised, formal, social or training events, simply offering to buy someone a coffee is a perfectly acceptable way of networking. In fact, by asking someone specifically to meet you, your networking is far more targeted to your small business needs than say larger group networking events. By asking someone to have coffee you are basically opening the door and saying "I'm interested in doing business with you" whether that be collaboration, sales or helping you to open the door to another person. I personally don't believe that there has to be a clear-cut outcome, collaboration or task from a coffee date as the meeting itself can be enough to motivate you. Nothing does more for my productivity and motivation than time out of my Harry Potter style hidey hole under the stairs home office, I mean there are NO windows! And time away from my business. Coffee provides the perfect opportunity to remind each other of your business and what you can offer or ways to collaborate. A study conducted by Regus (The Workplace Revolution, 2017) states that 54% of the world's workforce work outside the main office at least 2.5 days a week. So, what makes coffee shops appealing? They provide a relaxed, less stuffy corporate environment in which to run your small business or meet with potential collaborators, even clients. Coffee shops naturally put people at ease and provide a neutral space, which in turn increases honesty and creativity.

CO-WORKING SPACES AND UK JELLY

Co-working spaces are a shared workplace, usually a designated office, studio or cafe style environment which involves independent activity. However, unlike your typical, traditional type office, co-workers aren't employed by the same organisation, being made up generally of freelancers looking to get out of their home offices and reduce the loneliness factor. Co-working spaces provide variety within your working day, a change from the normal four walls, each environment has all the facilities needed (Wi-Fi, refreshments, desks, etc.) for freelancers to meet up with like-minded people and work together or just work in the same space where there are no expectations. A change in environment also increases focus whilst keeping remote workers/freelancers socially connected.

At co-working spaces, conversations will naturally progress, added to the fact that if you have chosen to work in a co-working space then you obviously crave some adult conversation and want to speak to other people otherwise you'd just hide at home, which means there is an inevitable exchange of ideas, help and advice, leading to possible new collaborations or progression in your own small business. Co-working, as trendy, current and up-to-date as it sounds, is in fact not a modern-day concept although with the number of freelance workers in the UK having reached over two million since 2001, it may seem like it. But in fact, back in 15th-century Florence, painters, sculptors, architects, engineers and scientists worked together in the Renaissance bottega. Bottega workshops often brought together different types of talent to compete, collaborate and nurture new talent, very much like our modern day co-working spaces.

Co-working spaces reduce the lure and distraction of your home (think household chores or in my case a lot of eating) instead providing you with a sense of discipline to your working day. There are also more practical aspects of co-working spaces including sharing insurance, childcare and other business-related services such as an admin assistant, mailing facility or meeting spaces so you can conduct meetings in a more professional environment. Many co-working spaces provide small businesses with complete flexibility; you are able to hire and utilise the facilities as little or often as you need. Loneliness is a recurrent theme within this book as working from home is at times very lonely, co-working spaces help to combat that sense of isolation self-employed people often experience providing a safe place to network, gain new contacts and ultimately work at the same time. If you are new to networking or less confident in large group situations, welcome speeches/60-second pitches then a co-working space may work better for you. Co-working spaces still provide you with the opportunity to build up relationships, develop your support network and find potential clients, collaborators or suppliers.

Whilst there are many, many branded co-working spaces there's absolutely nothing wrong with a coffee shop, free Wi-Fi and a group of small business friends. Or consider looking into your local Jelly. What exactly is a Jelly? A Jelly is an informal co-working weekly or monthly event where freelancers, home workers and small business owners turn up with their current workload, chat and collaborate with other small business owners. Established in 2006 by a couple of New York freelancers who were discussing how one major drawback of working from home is the sheer lack of company. They decided to invite a group of freelancers to bring their laptops and work together in their apartment for the day, and called it Jelly due to eating jelly beans at the time! Inspired!

Jellys are designed to be accessible to all no matter the size of your business meaning as much as possible the venue, Wi-Fi and parking are provided free of charge; however, food and drink is available if required at the normal venue fee. Jellys differ from more formal based organised networking events as the aim is not to find new clients or to sell yourself or your small business, the emphasis is placed upon literally completing your current tasks at hand/to-do list but with the added option of conversation. Never underestimate how productive you can be working away from the house. Working away from your home office provides you with headspace, a chance for clearer thinking enabling you to feel far more focused. Having this timeout from you usual working environment means you also prioritise the time more effectively than in your office where you might flounder about and get distracted. Time blocking is such an effective tool in getting things done and boosting productivity.

What is time blocking? The basic idea is that you schedule your whole day, including breaks, mealtimes, business and other activities throughout your working day. Block frequency and duration is based upon personal preference but most people opt for either 25 minutes of work and a five-minute break, or 50 minutes of work and a 10-minute break. Remember to also schedule in your personal time too, otherwise you know you won't take any.

The Swedish also have a co-working system, which is currently making its way through the UK, in comparison to co-working spaces and Jelly. Hoffice has a more structured and disciplined approach. The aim of the Hoffice network is to create free work spaces, by utilising an underused resource during-the-day – our homes. Unlike a Jelly, Hoffice has a structured timetable to the day which enables the attendees to benefit from the support of the collective freelancers but at the same time work individually on their own project. According to research Hoffice suggests that people are unable to concentrate for more than 45 minutes at a time, as such the timetable is broken down into 45-minute shifts. When the shift ends, an alarm clock buzzes, and the group takes a short break to exercise or meditate. Before the next 45-minute shift starts, everyone explains what they hope to achieve by the break; this adds a little social pressure and accountability to actually accomplish something because, let's face it, who wants to get to the end of the shift and not have completed your task? As Hoffice lasts all day everyone is also encouraged to bring food to share for a potluck lunch, eating is a social activity therefore it goes without saying that conversation will naturally and organically progress.

NETWALKING

As previously mentioned in Chapter Two, the health benefits for walking are vast, add that to the benefits of networking and well Netwalking for me is a winning combination. I run a monthly 'Netwalking' but I know of other walking events for small business owners locally including "Beach Walk and Talk", Netwalk or NetWALK, the emphasis being on walking whilst networking. Netwalking is also the easiest thing to set up yourself if there isn't anything locally already, as you are literally walking, there is no financial outlay to you or the attendees. I live on the edge of the New Forest so this works well for us. Use your local surroundings, the sea, the moors, Country Parks. If you have to drive quite far people may be less inclined to attend. Invite other small business acquaintances. The easiest way is to set up an event on your Facebook Business Page, share in networking groups and see what happens. If nobody turns up then at least you get out for a walk yourself (always looking for a positive = happy small business owner). Freelancers and small business owners are in a unique position whereby we are able to take a couple of hours away from our desks in order to enjoy the fresh air but still able to build our network. My group usually meets at 10am and we finish our route between 11:30/12 depending on how long we stop for coffee but also how large the group is. Larger groups walk a lot slower I have discovered.

Netwalking provides you with an opportunity to work on your business whilst walking, whereas we generally spend a lot of time working in our business. Netwalking has fast become one of my favourite monthly networking events. I love getting out in the New Forest (Shrin Roku inspired) absorbing nature the sights, smells and sounds of the passing seasons. But I also love meeting up with other business owners, chatting about what has happened in their business since we last met. We walk at a brisk pace but one at which we can still chat to each other, as a low impact exercise walking is accessible to everyone, which includes children and dogs making Netwalking a great event to catch up with small business owners during school holidays.

One of the major concerns for me about working from home is the isolation, which in turn can affect our wellbeing and cause unnecessary stress. Walking boosts our stress-easing endorphins and talking provides us with an opportunity to say things out loud which in turn can often make them appear less scary. Talking over your business problems, worries, issues or ideas releases tension that can build up – leading to stress and burnout. Talking with people outside your small business who don't know the day to day intricacies provides you with an unbiased more objective perspective, new ideas and clearer thinking as they aren't overwhelmed by being in your business. The more you talk the more ideas are bounced around, they may also have solutions or suggestions you hadn't thought of. I really believe the act of being outside and walking stimulates a more natural flow of conversation far easier than in some more traditional formal networking settings.

Let's not forget the health benefits of walking. We spend a great deal of our time in a sedentary position sat (or standing) at a desk, hunched over a mobile phone or tablet. Walking is a great way to increase your activity without getting sweaty or out of breath. Walking reduces fatigue and increases circulation, all in turn improving your heart health. There is also an increase in your energy levels, metabolism, self-esteem and ultimately all this improves your mood. Nature and being outdoors has restorative properties, such as increasing your short-term memory and reducing stress. Even just a 30-minute walk can make a huge difference to your productivity.

WHAT IS MINDFULNESS AND WHY IS IT RELEVANT IN NETWORKING?

Mindfulness is one of those buzzwords, popular at the moment but what exactly is it? Mindfulness is a heightened awareness of your surroundings, paying more attention, without judgement and living at a slower, gentler pace. Mindfulness is a powerful psychological tool enabling people to respond calmly to situations. Walking is a perfect mindful activity.

PEDALTALK

If walking isn't your thing, I have heard of other innovative networking groups out there, something to suit the needs, interests and hobbies of everyone. PedalTalk for example combines cycling and connecting with like-minded business professionals in beautiful countryside. We bring together groups of business people to enhance their professional and referral network. The bike provides the time and head-space to meet and get to know new business contacts and cycling friends, PedalTalk cycle networking enables you to mix business with pleasure.

"I have always used networking as a tool to build my referral network. And have been lucky enough to find new clients from my networking efforts.

It always surprises me how many people didn't network due to them not being comfortable walking into a room, that's potentially full of strangers, and striking up a conversation, or joining in to an existing group and/or conversation. I believe PedalTalk helps break down some of these barriers as most people already have a shared interest; cycling.

'PedalTalk absolutely champions business networking, PedalTalk shifts the standard expectation of suits, hotel boardrooms and bland breakfasts … to fresh air, bikes and a true sense of shared experience.

We bring together groups of business people to enhance their professional and referral network. The bike gets people away from their mobile and provides the time, and head-space, to meet and get to know new business contacts and cycling friends.

Some of the reasons people attend a PedalTalk event: to benefit from new ideas, openly discuss current challenges, build relationships, increase their visibility, enhance their referral network, for some it helps them re-find work motivation, and obviously everyone gets to ride bikes."

Darren Blackstock, PedalTalk

SELF-EMPLOYED TEAM BUILDING SOCIALS

I touched on Self-employed Team Building Socials in Chapter Two but what exactly are they, what do they entail and what is it really all about? I started these socials events on a bit of a whim in January 2018 and now hold a regular monthly event with a core team of small business owners who come every time, some that dip in and out, but always with new people joining at each event. Occasionally the best ideas just develop organically by themselves rather than being forced and over planned. Although Self-employed Team Building Socials are slightly indulgent on my part as I'm able to organise fun activities, learn new skills I'd like to develop whilst encouraging my small business friends to join me. What's not to love?!

OK, just kidding there is actually a lot more to Self-employed Team Building Socials and the best bit is anyone can set something like this up. Unlike traditional more formal networking situations, there is no expectation placed upon you from others in the group. This isn't a sales opportunity, there's no round robin, pitch session (of course if it's your first time everyone is bound to ask you about who you are, what you do, etc.). You can relax, just be yourself, have fun; conversations will inevitably and naturally progress and develop. Getting out of the office, to be able to be actively encouraged to completely switch off from work, whilst engaging in something fun is good for the soul. Mental health and how we feel is something we well and truly underestimate and comradery when working alone is something we crave. Self-employed Team Building Socials make me happy. Happiness increases productivity. What more can I say?

> *"Loving the sessions so far. Having a bit of 'me' time and getting out of the day to day business stuff has been great. Being self-employed can feel a bit lonely at times, but having some social events to attend has been great for my health and wellbeing. Thank you!"*
>
> *Trisha Reece: Virtual PA Services*

When you initially think team building, you probably think about corporate days out and in some cases, we do engage in many of those activities, archery, abseiling, fencing we even went trampolining once! The idea of corporate team building sessions are to take a group of individual employees who work together interdependently and cooperatively and looks at turning this group of individuals into a cohesive team, through activities. Being self-employed / freelancers, we can easily become hermits and forget how to interact with others. Whilst we may no longer need to build our team these skills really are vital. Of course, being small business owners' conversations always gravitate towards business. It's also a great opportunity to talk openly about things that might be stressing you out, other great events and courses you have been to.

> *"I love the team spirit – it's great to want to do well for yourself but even better to be cheered on by the other attendees."*
>
> *Jackie Richmond, Lemur Landings.*

Choose to spend time with people who lift you up rather than bring you down; those who make you feel seen, heard and important. I feel proud to have developed a network that supports my small business but also supports my health and wellbeing. I choose to surround myself with the encouragers, not the critics. Toxic people and friendships will bring you down. I've not been to one Self-employed Team Building Social or Netwalking event where I haven't been surrounded by happiness, laughter and smiling faces. Building a network/support/tribe around you will only make you stronger.

"I love meeting other freelancers for social get-together as it means I get away from my desk and have some fun. I feel more motivated afterwards."

Anne Cornish, Anne Cornish Virtual Assistant.

CONFERENCES AND TRADE SHOWS

Conferences and industry-based trade shows work wonders in developing your business knowledge and meeting experts within your industry. When I attended Sage Summit in 2017, I knew a few people but not everyone going. Using the designated hashtag #SageSummit on Twitter I was able to find other attendees staying in my hotel, I even met one for drinks the evening before. Using social media, I organised to meet other attendees for breakfast and to travel together to the venue. Pre-prep is important, organising your agenda, where you want to go, brands, businesses you want to meet, seminars you want to watch and read through the floor plan get to know the layout. These little things will make the whole experience less daunting and there's strength in numbers, as they say. Use social media to your advantage to connect with the right people during the event.

GENRE SPECIFIC

Many small business genres actively meet up to network together, virtual assistants, photographers, professional coaches, bloggers to name a few. They don't see themselves as competition rather as complementary to each other. For example, VAs (virtual assistant) benefit from networking together as they can't possibly ever possess every skill required by every client, in every given situation. Working together in this way eliminates the idea of competition, instead fostering and promoting a sense of community. I like communities. I like the idea of building something around myself that is bigger and better than just me. A community of VAs working together in order to serve other small business owners rather than working against each other, looks like the ultimate win-win of networking to me.

Bloggers always hang out and network together, brands actually organise their events with networking opportunities for bloggers as the main aim. By networking together bloggers are able to share skills, contacts and work through issues they may have from web design to search engine optimisation. Again, if there isn't something local to you, genre specific, start one!

FINAL THOUGHT

Even if your small business appears niche compared to others within your local area, networking and meeting other small business owners is vital. Regardless of your industry at some point all small businesses will experience the same issues in some way or another. By networking and communicating with others within different genres and industries you bring variety and varied perspectives to the group.

Running a small business from home, for me, is a means to achieve a family friendly flexible work-life balance therefore time is a precious commodity. Anything that requires leaving the office has to be a worthwhile investment in your business and that includes leaving it for a cup of coffee and a chat. You don't want to be involved with or attend networking events that do not enhance your business in any way. Remember, enhancing your business is not the same as selling, enhancing looks at building your tribe/support network, learning new skills, collaborating with others and growing your business and making you happy as happiness = productive people. If the networking group isn't hitting one of those key factors then I would chalk it up to experience and move on, there will always be other events better suited to you personally, your small business and its needs. Finding appropriate and effective networking events and/or networking groups is all down to trial and error. You will always need to try a few as one size does not fit all.

"I had a TERRIBLE experience. People felt pressured into presenting/pitching in a particular way, and as showing themselves to be wildly successful; no vulnerability allowed. Also, instead of openly asking for referrals or asking if interested, there was lots of salesy stuff going on. Awkward! So, I started my own group, it was very friendly and welcoming and had an open ethos. For example, that there was no competition between people, only different people attracting different clients, we shared our knowledge and experience freely, supported each other, shared the difficulties in our businesses and how that reflected our personal process. It was safe; good boundaries, no gossip. There was and still is a lot of collaboration, projects, working together that spontaneously happened. We ran workshops to support our businesses, personal growth and clients' issues. I no longer do monthly meetings."

Kate Codrington

CHAPTER FOUR

PREPARATION

O nce you find a networking group that meets your lifestyle needs and small business requirements, i.e. time, venue, price, there is still that undeniable fear of having to 'sell' yourself and ultimately your small business. Well guess what? Networking isn't about selling yourself at all (if you didn't get that point in the first three chapters). In fact, and I really will start to sound like a broken record, networking is about developing relationships and making connections within your local small business community. Networking is part of the long game providing you with a lot more substantial business pros than a quick five-minute sale. In the lead up to a networking event, how you prepare including starting to make connections can be advantageous to the outcome of the event and ultimately how confident you feel when you get there. Preparation is really important. Proper preparation will leave you feeling calm and confident both emotionally and with regards to your small business.

PITCH PERFECT

Inigo Montoya, The Princess Bride Film (1987)

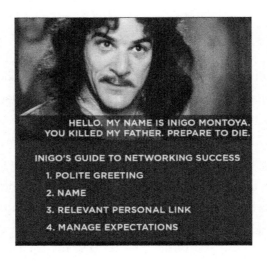

HELLO. MY NAME IS INIGO MONTOYA.
YOU KILLED MY FATHER. PREPARE TO DIE.

INIGO'S GUIDE TO NETWORKING SUCCESS
1. POLITE GREETING
2. NAME
3. RELEVANT PERSONAL LINK
4. MANAGE EXPECTATIONS

Consider putting together an elevator pitch. Now I know this sounds like I'm contradicting myself suggesting that networking isn't about selling by insisting you need an elevator pitch but this is really to do with confidence and understanding rather than sales. Think of your elevator pitch more in terms of "Hello my name is ..." followed by a sentence or two about your business, ensuring you have a clear understanding of what you do and what your small business benefits are to others. A good elevator pitch is your offline equivalent of a really well curated social media post. In the same way that you strive to ensure that your social media post promotes curiosity and encourages engagement with your followers and target audience, your elevator pitch needs to do the same. A survey of 2,000

Canadians in 2015 by the Consumer Insights team of Microsoft Canada concluded that the average attention span had fallen to eight seconds, down from 12 in the year 2000. Officially shorter than that of a goldfish! If you cannot easily or eloquently tell people what your small business is and does then others will struggle to know, understand or even see the benefit to them (or others). Think about the language you use, try to avoid words such as 'just, little business, only,' which makes you sound tentative, lacking in confidence and ultimately unsure. Our language shapes our perspective and that of those we are addressing.

Example: I 'just' write a blog about business vs I write a multi awarding winning small business blog. This enabled me to write an Amazon bestseller and work with companies such as Sage UK as a small business expert.

Using 'just' as an adverb describing how you do something, makes it sound like I'm unsure whereas the definite 'I write' resonates the fact I understand my business and my role.

> *'The difference between the right word and the almost right word is the difference between lightning and a lightning bug.'*
>
> *Mark Twain*

Or consider flipping your 'elevator pitch' on its head by focusing on the results of what you do, not just the definition of your small business. Alexia Browning, Made By Me Craft Parties: "*I used to feel really awkward about presenting myself and small business at Lemur Linkup until I was introduced to the idea of elevator pitches. I worked through what the key points of my business were and now I say "My name is Lexy, I own award-winning Made By Me Craft Parties. I run beautiful, fun and personalised craft parties for children, teens and adults." It's made me so much more confident as I have a clearer idea about what exactly I'm going to say."*

Avoid pompous, industry jargon, which is both unnatural, not at all authentic and will always leave the person you're talking to feeling confused. End with a call to action if you can, so that the listener knows exactly what to do next. Repeat the main message for example: "My name is Joanne, I create and design handmade fabric party bags and sell a range of quirky party supplies".

PRACTICE MAKES PERFECT

Practice your elevator pitch so that it easily rolls off the tongue and you really believe it, feel it and it's not just a jumble of words you strung together to sound semi-professional. Consider tailoring your pitch to match your surroundings, the industries and small business genres at each networking events. This shows that you have done your research and have something useful to offer/provide for the other attendees and their clients/customers or possible collaborations. Define a problem and a solution using your pitch to show how you and your small business can solve the problem both efficiently and effectively. Establishing a USP (unique selling point) to help you stand out from others in your industry, underscores the value you will bring to other small businesses within your networking circle and beyond. Always revisit your elevator pitch to include any changes to your small business, seasonal changes or any business awards or achievements you have received.

KEY POINTS

- Identify your goal.
- Explain what you do.
- Communicate your USP.
- Engage with a question.
- Put it all together.
- Practice.

NETWORKING KIT

Never assume things will be readily available to you at networking events. Always pack yourself a kit which includes a pen, consider also taking a Sharpie in case you want to write notes on business cards as many people will have luxurious glossy ones and a normal pen won't work, paper/notebook and your business cards or current flyers.

If you are a content creator will you need any additional equipment such as a mobile phone, camera, additional lights or microphones. During Sage UK events many of the attendees are social influencers/content creators and will spend time creating short videos, live streaming or memes of the event.

The night before events make sure you have all the items ready and packed. I find it useful after networking events to clear my bag. This way you take action, sort through business cards, find contacts on social media or send them an email straight away rather than finding them crumpled months later.

BUSINESS CARD

I recently went to a networking event where I talked about blogging, and a guy who ran a small printing business said he had no idea what to write about. I replied with 'Are business cards dead or still a useful tool?' As it happened every attendee at that event had some to hand out but this isn't usually the norm. Many people don't see business cards as a necessity as it's easy to say 'Oh I'm JoanneDewberryUK across the board on social media.' *cough blatant plug cough* but unless you follow them straight away (i.e. right THEN at the event, which most people won't) you may just forget. A business card works as a physical reminder that you met someone, their details and most importantly what they do. I believe business cards are an essential piece of your marketing and networking kit (and if you haven't got any left consider taking along your latest flyer, special offer posters, class list or do you publish a magazine?). I currently have 250 mini 2020 calendars with my face on (no word of a lie). Take anything tangible that you can give away to new people you meet. Always carry something. Business cards also make you look far more professional and organised; it's a little bit lame scratching your details down on a scrap of paper or being disorganised with nothing at all to share. The hardest part, when it comes to business cards, is deciding just what information you should include on the cards. It can be easy to overload the business card with tons of information as mentally you don't want to miss anything but as a receiver this can look really busy and give the receiver far too many options. Too many options can also make it hard for the receiver to know what you do and what you want them to do, call to actions are important but too many is overwhelming.

Contact Details: Email, phone, website and most importantly your name. It's always the obvious things we overlook. Don't overload your business card with social media platforms, pick one and remember we always have our phones to hand - you can always ask them 'What's your Twitter handle and I'll follow you now". It's also a handy way to keep the conversation flowing. But don't worry; as once you start connecting with individuals offline you can always direct them to other platforms.

What You Do: Unless your business name gives away your job description (i.e. Samantha Prewett Photography, Jo's Face Painting where it is obvious to the reader what you do, then it is a waste of space adding it) it doesn't matter how gorgeous your business card is if doesn't say what you do it's a wasted opportunity. It doesn't need to be War and Peace just a snippet of information, your tagline or occupation. I use Joanne Dewberry, UK Small Business Blogger

Use the Front and Back: I always think it looks unfinished or like you ran out of money when you don't use both sides of a business card. The back is great for adding information or images, if you sell products or are a photographer. Moo.com allows you to upload more than one image enabling you to showcase your business. It can also be handy for targeting your audience. For example, a photographer may choose to give out his head shot images at a corporate networking event and save his weddings images for a wedding suppliers networking event or family orientated for mums in business-based industry. Or why not use the backs of business cards as loyalty or appointment cards, this technique will ensure people hold onto them longer too.

Think Quality: Always opt for the best quality you can afford. Be careful though, as some cheaper printers may request their branding or website address on your business cards as a way of providing them at that low cost price. If you have a handmade business there really isn't anything wrong with making your own business cards, however remember to consider if this will be cost effective. Make sure your business card sparkles and shouts quality; this in turn creates a lasting impression, for example, soft touch laminate is tactile and anyone who receives it will feel it, spending time reading because the quality feels nice. If you take this much care over your business card imagine what the receiver will be thinking about the quality of your service. We are judgmental people and the first interaction you have with someone will have a bearing on what people think.

Does your business card fit in a holder?: Always make sure your business card fits into a business card holder. When you are passing business cards to each other the last thing you want is someone putting it into their bag rather than their neat holder because it's too large. The business card is likely to be disposed of if it's not already ruined rolling round in their bag alongside half a bag of sweets, a leaking bottle of water, unpaid bills and their long lost dreams. Or is that just the bottom of my bag!?

Format: Do not automatically assume business cards should be landscape. Why not stand out from the crowd, present something different and design your business card in portrait.

Think About the Colour: Some people might want to jot details down on your business card, clues to remind them about your small business maybe where you met for when they get home. In this case I'd try to avoid dark or block colours like blue and black. Personally, I think you can't go wrong with at least one side being more white, simplistic possibly slightly more minimalistic.

Avoid Using Templates: Ensure your business card is unique to you and not one off the shelf that looks like everyone else's.

Streamline Your Branding: Retail expert and fellow Sage UK Business Expert Graham Soult, Canny Insights, has designed his business cards in the style of retail Top Trumps, not only is this in keeping with his branding, it's a talking point and it makes his cards memorable (otherwise I wouldn't be mentioning it now). Streamline your branding by sticking to exact colours, fonts and images which are all synonymous with your small business brand.

Update and Re-evaluate Business Cards Regularly: Things chang. Fact. You don't want to be turning up to an event with an out of date business card. You may change your business name, phone number, email or even your physical address if you have premises.

VIRTUAL BUSINESS CARDS

Of course, it wouldn't be the new modern technology-based era without virtual business cards. Yup you heard me right, a virtual business card enables individuals you meet to scan it to become a subscriber or find out all there is to know about you and your small business – removing the need to take business cards that they may never use or lose. Virtual business cards are efficient, green and effective. Saving paper increases your green credentials but also saving your small business money and it's handy to know this technology exists just in case you run out of traditional business cards, forget them or go to an event last minute. I guess it's like most things your feelings will be based on personal preference. If you like receiving physical items and the more personal touch you are more likely to gravitate towards a business card however if you love tech and the latest gadgets, you're more likely to prefer the virtual version. Personally, I prefer paper, I love gluing and sticking. I love creating collages and using business cards in my bullet journal/goal setting book and physical cards stick in your mind where a digital transfer doesn't. It is handy to consider both and their availability so your new contact can make their own decision.

It is really easy to set up virtual business cards yourself through Facebook Messenger on your Facebook Small Business Page. You are able to share your digital business card directly to a person's Facebook account from Facebook Messenger. The digital business card will appear in the individual's inbox. There are plenty of tutorials online showing you how to create one.

PERSONAL BRANDING

> *"Your smile is your logo, your personality is your business card, how you leave others feeling after an experience with you becomes your trademark."*
>
> *Jay Danzie*

Personal branding is probably not the top of your list but remember we buy from people we like so how you present yourself is really important. Your personal brand is not only reflected by what we do or look like (again we are judgemental people) but also by what others feel about what you do.

You can't really discuss personal branding without looking at clothing. For some small business owners, they may already wear a uniform or branded T-shirt, however others use clothing as an extension of their business brand. *"My brand colours are magenta pink and gunmetal grey. The grey is a strong/safe colour while the magenta pink is known for instilling confidence. When I launched my VA business, I wanted people to have confidence that I was a safe pair of hands for their business. I always wear clothing in these colours to networking*

82

events." Amanda Johnson, Virtual Assistant Coaching and Training.

Do you think about what you wear? I wouldn't turn up in a suit but at the same time I wouldn't turn up in my pj's! You have to be comfortable but also you have to be authentic.

SOCIAL MEDIA PRESENCE

How often have you been to a networking event where someone greets you like an old friend and you have absolutely no idea who they are because they use their small business logos or a bitmoji (a cartoon avatar of yourself or personal emoji) as their social media avatars? It's cringeworthy, you either have to keep talking until you figure it out or ask them to remind you what line of business they are in, either way hoping it jogs some memory. Also, as freelancers, self-employed individuals we ARE our business. We ARE our brand. I use my own name (Joanne Dewberry – in case you need reminding – across the board on all social media platforms. I look forward to the new follow!). This is becoming more and more popular with freelancers as our name is the most unique part of our business which people can connect and identify with. I use an actual photograph of myself, which I had professionally taken as an investment in my business, the same for all my social media avatars which ensures instant recognition. We aren't a logo we are real people. I change my hair colour a lot, so I always try and use an updated image. Sometimes it's the obvious things we don't realise which make a massive impact.

83

NAME BADGES

Not all events will supply one therefore consider having one made or a lanyard that you can put your business card into. If you do wear a name badge the best position is on the left-hand side making it in clear visual line when shaking someone's hand. You will find the majority of people are right-handed, when putting a label or badge on it is far easier to attach to the left-hand side. You will also find most branded uniforms/t-shirts will have the logo on the left. The best name badges use a clear and large font alongside your small business name and your first name – although this seems obvious, too often it's actually very hard to tell who is actually who at an event. Being able to quickly eyeball a company name and first name without appearing obvious, knowing who to speak to and introducing yourself becomes much simpler. Also, if your business or social media is under a different name to you add this as some people might not recognise your actual name. You may also choose to wear branded clothing, T-shirts, etc. which then become part of your networking uniform and instantly recognisable to others.

THINGS TO DO BEFORE A NETWORKING EVENT

Pre-prep: Preparation is key to feeling confident and avoiding awkwardness. Knowing some basic information will help you to feel more in control. For example:

- How will you get there? Car, train, bus, walk?
- Where can you park and do you need change for the parking

machine?

- Where is the meeting room?
- Will there be refreshments? If food is served have you let the organisers know of any dietary requirements?
- Where are the nearest toilets?
- Do you have your networking kit?

Some events will also provide you with an attendance list including name and business details, if these aren't available (our Lemur Linkup events are so informal we don't require people to book in advance) then look to see if the event is on Facebook. Find out who else is attending, once you have a name or business name you will be able to look them up on Twitter or find their Facebook Business Page, simply introduce yourself. It's a really easy and less scary way to get to know somebody a little. Knowing someone will reduce your nerves, increase your confidence but also provide conversation starters.

Join Facebook groups, most networking groups will have an online presence, filled with like-minded small business owners and freelancers, this works as a way to ease yourself in, it can be a lot easier to communicate virtually. In fact, there are networking groups on Facebook for literally everything; you can make connections with people all over the world. I recommend joining a variety of groups – a collection of local, worldwide and industry based. Local networking groups on Facebook can be invaluable if you are anxious or a bit of an introvert. The Facebook online groups can be a great way to dip a toe in the water. You are able to introduce yourself and your business from the comfort of your home, make connections and ultimately start to get to know people using the group beforehand, which really helps you to feel more comfortable on your first visit. Facebook groups help you to get a feel for the group; the online group also helps to continue face to face conversations, note sharing and information. I've lost count of the amount of times I remember things or have a blog post relevant to a situation/conversation. Having a Lemur Linkup Facebook group provides somewhere to share these things that might otherwise get forgotten.

Using a hashtag online usually works better on Twitter or Instagram (for Lemur Linkup we use #lemurchat), and can make it easier to locate content and people from networking sessions. As there are a couple of us hosting each Lemur Linkup event and also the speaker there is usually someone tweeting snippets, golden nuggets of content throughout the session. This not only helps you find specific people after the event but also enables you to feel like part of the conversation if you are unable to personally attend.

Take a small business friend or colleague (but not your mum) with you on your first networking outing. There is something to be said about using the buddy system, yes even though we are grown-up business professionals, inviting a friend to go to an event with you is an automatic guarantee of moral support (actual hand holding is optional). Instead of walking into a room of complete strangers, you'll have a companion who can help spark conversations and ease you out of awkward moments and make you feel more confident than standing alone. Plus, if the event ends up being not what you had anticipated, at least you'll be hanging out with someone you really like.

Knowing who is there and something about their small business enables you to take the lead in a conversation, it leaves you feeling confident with new people. But just remember that even with ice breakers, be yourself and stay authentic. Conversation is an art. Don't force a joke or start conversations about things you don't know about because you set yourself up to fail, look silly and feel awkward. Never underestimate the power of "small talk", the weather or the venue – these are shared experiences that anyone you speak to will be able to relate to.

Use any delegate list or Facebook event to make goals. Are there certain people/small businesses you have identified that you could collaborate or work with? If so ask for an introduction. In situations where you're going to an event with colleagues or clients, ask them to introduce you to people who you've been wanting to meet or who intimidate you. By allowing other people to introduce you to new faces, the people you're meeting will be more likely to acknowledge you and engage in conversation since you already have something in common. Furthermore, having a third-party present during the conversation leaves less pressure on everyone involved to carry on a discussion.

Chapter Five

Communication and Body Language

"The only thing we have to fear is fear itself"

Franklin D. Roosevelt

'm not going to lie, but IT IS daunting walking into a room and meeting people, maybe not even for the first time. Even now I still get a few butterflies when someone new walks into Lemur Linkup or I go somewhere I've never been before. If you can, arrange to meet a colleague or online buddy there beforehand to ease your nerves, or find out if the event is on Facebook or has a delegate list so you are a little more prepared. Once I enter a room, I usually have a scan round to see if there is someone I know personally or have chatted with before on social media to walk over and sit next to or generally just say hi.

Once in the room, it's really important to learn to read and interpret people's body language and the situation, a skill we are becoming completely rubbish at. For example; two people who are talking closely together probably don't want to be interrupted as they are closing themselves off from the group, however, if these two people are standing side by side facing into the room, then this is an invitation to come and join them.

Watch out for people that are standing on their own, they can usually be found looking really busy around the buffet or coffee facilities, but they actually want to be approached. If on the other hand that person feeling nervous is you then lurking close to the coffee facilities is the place to position yourself. Most people will head for drinks on arrival and anyone heading straight for coffee already has something in common with you, making it easier to spark up a conversation. *"Have you come far?"* or *"I really need this coffee today"* – the usual small talk which can easily be followed up by *"My name is Joanne Dewberry, I write a UK Small Business Blog. What about you?"* By being the first to ask a question or engage in conversation allows you a moment of calm, they are talking about themselves therefore you don't have to worry about what to say. A bit of back and forth questioning, chit/chat, small talk is a great way to start a conversation and learn something about that person.

Think about your body language, adopting a few handy techniques can increase your confidence, put you at ease and take the stress out of networking. We are all so consumed with online transactions these days that reading body language and face to face communication is a dying art and skill most of us lack. I know it takes me a few minutes to ease in, which is why I like to turn up to Lemur Linkup early. I warm myself up with small talk with the soft play staff and Jackie, the co-host, so by the time attendees start arriving we are fuelled by coffee and raring to go.

> *"I've learned that people will forget what you said, people will forget what you did, but people will never forget how you made them feel."*
>
> *Maya Angelou*

Be yourself: Social Influencers (vloggers, bloggers, professional Instagrammers, yup that's a real thing!) talk about being authentic, this is a fancy way of saying be yourself, not trying to adopt a persona which ultimately you are unlikely to be able to carry through indefinitely. Could you pretend long term to be someone else? The answer is probably no, so it's better to just be yourself. When my daughter started middle school and there were suddenly 150 children her age rather than a class of 25, she found it hard to be herself through worry people wouldn't like her. We adults are exactly the same, people pleasers. With the rise of social media now more than ever, WE are our brand as much as the colours and logo are. Be transparent. You want to make sure your voice, your values, and your personality shine through in all that you do.

3 WAYS TO STAY AUTHENTIC IN YOUR SMALL BUSINESS

1. **Love what you do**: You will never grow your small business if you don't have any passion or enthusiasm for the business genre you are in. On many occasions it is this passion and enthusiasm which increases your likeability and attracts your network/support group/tribe rather than your products/small business itself. Loving your small business will also provide you with clarity, about who and what you are/do, enabling you to create sustainable long-term connections, rather than one off sales.

92

2. **Keeping it real**: This is especially true when you share details of your life and/or business online, running a small business around a family and by yourself is not always easy and believe me it's rarely Instagram perfect. We all make mistakes but using these mistakes to grow, develop and help others avoid them not only provides evidence of the human side of the business but makes you more relatable to others around you.

3. **Believe**: You have to have belief in yourself, your values and stick with them. Never feel like you have to change yourself or agree with people for the sake of it. Don't be a people pleaser.

BODY LANGUAGE FOR COMMUNICATION

Smile and the world smiles with you: Your smile is one of, if not the best asset you have and you don't even need to look for it or pack it in your bag! Smiling opens up your eyes and face, this in turn instantly makes you look approachable and kind. Unless of course you smile awkwardly like my pre-teen son who ends up looking a bit stalkerish or that he possibly needs the toilet. Smiling shows confidence and opens the way for communication making those around you feel more comfortable.

Be approachable: Fake confidence, keep eye contact and respond to the person speaking to you as this not only indicates you are engaged and interested but keeps the conversation flowing. Listen more than you talk and actively take an interest in people and what they do.

Actively listen: Allow people to speak first, not only is it very polite and very British, but you are basically saying "I'm interested in what you have to say" which makes the speaker feel good. This form of listening requires you as the listener to fully concentrate, understand, respond and then remember what is being said – unlike reflective listening whereby the listener repeats what they have just heard to confirm understanding for both parties. Actively listening is a communication technique that is used in counselling, training, and conflict resolution. Always listen and engage with the content, don't be thinking how can I jump in and make it about me and my small business. Active listening helps conversations to flow better and keep those conversations flowing. Flowing conversations will in turn increase your confidence.

Being present is also a key component when networking and vital to active listening. Being present within the conversation, not daydreaming about other things, not wondering when you can interject with your comment, not thinking about the buffet that has just arrived, being completely and utterly present in the conversation as it happens.

Throughout any conversations you have to actively listen, be present and engage. By listening, you build up a level of trust and authority. You can then use this authority to position yourself as an expert in your genre. By listening you are also able to think about ways that you or your wider network can add value to this small business, from collaboration to sales. Being able to add value to other small businesses soon makes you a crucial part of people's network and in

94

turn they become more receptive to helping you later when you may need it. Small business relationships develop naturally and organically and should not be forced, but taking the time to actively listen and engage will help foster these relationships.

"When you listen, do it for the sake of understanding and not just to build a reply"

www.teenwellbeing.co.uk

Body Language: Our body language is really important and something we can overlook. Albert Mehrabian's 7-38-55 Rule of Personal Communication concluded that 55% of communication is body language, 38% is the tone of voice, and 7% is the actual words spoken. Although this study was conducted in 1967, I think it's still relevant today. Our body language can say a lot about us and reading this is something we as a society have become unable to do, as far too much communication is conducted virtually. When you consider the 7-38-55 Rule of Personal Communication body language and tone of voice cannot be communicated online virtually even with emojis and gifs.

Think about the way you stand. Avoid crossing your arms in front of you as this can close you off and make you appear aggressive. I always naturally find myself crossing my arms so I try and find something to hold whether that be my bag, notebook or a cup of coffee, this way I give my hands a purpose and it stops my arms from crossing. The way in which someone stands, will make a difference in whether I feel comfortable to approach them myself. Be aware of the 'vibe' your body language gives off. In the same breath as previously mentioned always try and keep eye contact. Looking at the floor will make you feel and appear to others as nervous. When you come across as not confident others may struggle to see the value you and your small business will add to theirs. In group situations leave a physical gap between you and others, don't form a closed circle. This makes it easier for other individuals to join in with the conversation – the gap appears like an open invitation. A closed circle can look daunting, private and cut off.

The Power Position: Stand with your feet shoulder width apart, chin up, head high, hands on hips. Do this for a few minutes. The Power Position is known to increase assertiveness and confidence. Keep your hands out of your pockets, don't fiddle with things especially your phone, remember to keep eye-contact and actively listen and engage, you can't do this whilst tweeting.

Personal Branding: How are you going to stand out from the crowd? Personal branding is really important at networking events and it can also be your suit of armour. I mentioned in the previous chapter how Amanda Johnson, Virtual Assistant Coaching and Training, always carries or wears something that is magenta pink and/or gunmetal grey.

"My brand colours are magenta pink and gunmetal grey. The grey is a strong/safe colour while the magenta pink is known for instilling confidence. When I launched my VA business, I wanted people to have confidence that I was a safe pair of hands for their business." These colours have become part of Amanda's beliefs and business ethos; she literally believes that she is a safe pair of confident hands for her customers. This is prevalent in her personal branding. Do you know what your personal brand is? Does it identify what you and your small business stand for, your goals, motivation and the reason you choose to network?

Your personal branding also needs to be authentic. For example, if I was to turn up in a suit to a networking event, especially one I was co-hosting or speaking at, I'd feel awkward, uncomfortable and I'd probably behave in a manner that wasn't really me. In the same breath I'm unlikely to turn up to a Lemur Linkup in my pyjamas. I want to be relaxed but I also want to be taken seriously. I want to become more noticeable and attract people to me but for the right reasons.

Be proactive and ask open ended questions: There is nothing worse than when I pick my son up from school and I ask him about his day and he replies, "fine" or "OK". There is nowhere for me to go other than asking more questions which he soon gets annoyed with. Open ended questions stop the person you're talking with just replying with yes or no answers, meaning they have to construct and engage

97

in a discussion with you. This helps in turn to encourage conversations to flow. Don't stand around in the corner waiting for someone to talk to you either. If you've undertaken your research, you'll have a rough idea who is in the room and maybe already connected with someone online making the initial entrance much easier. Remember the Canadian study which concluded our attention span is shorter than a goldfish? Take that into consideration when asking and answering questions. Therefore, long in-depth answers or questions isn't going to work; eight seconds, dude! Always ensure your answers and questions are quick, jargon-free and informative without sounding over-rehearsed and/or contrived, but at the same time are engaging and keep conversation flowing. It's a lot easier than it sounds, promise.

Some people are great with names, others with faces; utilise both these facts. Remember someone. Remember something about their business, life, something you read on social media and ask them how it's going.

CHAPTER SIX

BUILDING RELATIONSHIPS

"My golden rule of networking is simple: don't keep score"

Harvey Mackay

've already touched on this but it's a hugely important factor within networking. The first thing you have to get into your mind straight away is that the key to networking lies within developing relationships. People need to know, like and trust you before they will engage in business with you or recommend you to all their friends. Networking is about building those key relationships and connections as discussed earlier that help you to grow your business.

"Business depends, utterly and completely, on relationships."

Michael Tobin 2018

When it comes to networking it is never what you know but WHO you know. Make connections, develop relationships, then these people will either do business with you or refer you to others. Networking isn't about selling a specific product or service to a room of individuals. Networking is not a quick fix to business success. Like anything in life, it can take time. Just like making friends saying hello once isn't going to make you best friends forever. You can't say you nailed social media marketing because you posted a link to your newest product on Twitter. In fairness that isn't really going to make you a sell-out. Networking and marketing take time and commitment. Commit to a group or meeting and stick with it. Going once, even twice, isn't enough. Go back time after time, take the time to nurture and grow those first-generation connections. If you find a group isn't working for you then try another. It's about finding what works and suits your small business.

Go with the intention of seeing who can you find business for. Who would add value to your service if you told your clients about that person? Look for people who will enhance your support network and help your small business grow, whether that be financially, through advice, or being an emotional crutch. With anything in life, think quality over quantity. It's better to have a small, active support network in which your small business is thriving, developing and growing than to attend every event in town whilst aggressively trying to sell with the main goal of thrusting as many business cards into as many hands as humanly possible. Plus, that's exhausting. The worst networking faux pas people make is paying little or no attention to anyone around them; this isn't a winning networking formula. There is nothing worse than turning up to an event and having someone talk at you about their small business for the umpteenth time because they didn't take the chance to chat to you properly previously, been an awful listener, not followed up online afterwards and therefore haven't even realised you have met before.

Don't get caught up in vanity networking. When we look at social media, we can easily get distracted by the numbers game, but again it is quality not quantity that counts. It is far better to have 200 followers who interact with you every day than 4000 who don't. This is the same with networking. A successful networking event isn't measured by the fact you have 25 business cards in your wallet. Some events provide you with an area to leave your business cards/flyers, enabling attendees to pick up cards from people they might have wanted to talk to but did not get the chance.

Spend time actually getting to know people really well, even if this is just a handful of people. Hand out business cards or leaflets when they are asked for. Never hard sell unless the group has a five-minute pitch/introduction session, and even then, as we looked at previously, this pitch is a way in which to introduce your small business with a clear understanding of what you do and what benefits you have to others. Leave the sales patter at home.

Having little, weak or even no relationships with others will inevitably have a high cost to small businesses, from personal happiness, business growth and development, as well as learning. Networking should always be a cornerstone of your business, developing relationships is key and then you will find business will follow naturally. As your confidence grows, you'll soon be able to broaden your networking circles to face to face events. Networking is also how I develop my support network/tribe/gang whatever word you want to use. I personally need these key people; they basically keep me sane and inspire me to push myself further. They hold me accountable to my goals and listen to me when I'm down. They aid my learning and development and they refer me to other small businesses. We buy from people we like, and more importantly, we recommend people we like. We need to get out there and talk to people. Be liked by others who will go on to say positive things about you to others: you never know, someone you meet this way might have just the connection you need to grow your business further.

Jim Rohn, an American entrepreneur, author and motivational speaker, once said that "*You are the sum of the five people you hang around with the most.*"

The implication of his statement is that you need to surround yourself with people who are as motivated as you. If you only stick within your circles it will be much harder to grow your small business and personal development. Powerful and purposeful networking increases the number of small business opportunities and enables you to build a network full of thoughtful and helpful people. We tend to stick to our own kind, we gravitate towards people just like us, however research shows that when we expose ourselves to a more diverse group of people we give "*the brain a powerful workout. And, just like a physical workout, it can be incredibly good for us.*" (BBC News, Crossing Divides, 2019).

Follow-up

According to Urbandictionary.com the literal meaning of "*I'll call you*" is "*I do not plan on calling you, EVER.*" I guess with online networking and social media the actual act of picking up a phone and calling people is becoming less and less the done thing. Or is this an indication that we just say things we don't really mean anymore. If you say you're going to call, take the time to call even if it's just to have a coffee and a chat. You won't want to collaborate, work or do business with everyone you meet but if you do think they are someone with whom you could start a working relationship, let them know. It's not very English to be bolshie and in someone's face, it also makes me feel really uncomfortable, so softly, softly works the best for both them and me. Send an email saying how good it was to meet them, reference something or someone from the event to help trigger memories from the day. I don't know about you but I'm so busy with the children after school and life that days sometimes merge into one long week. Explain why you think you might be a good match, or what kind of opportunity/collaboration you had in mind, ask for a chat over coffee or to bear you in mind for future opportunity.

You get out of networking what you put into it. Simple. If you want to develop strong networking relationships and build your support network then continuity and follow-up are key.

Continuity: Attend the same events; don't be a one hit wonder. In the beginning it's good to go to a few different events as some you'll like and others you won't, but once you find a couple you like stick with them.

Follow-up: You need to use this to continue developing relationships online as well as off. In some cases, the follow-up is just as important as networking itself, otherwise what is the point? Are you literally going to wait until the next networking event to take the relationship/conversation any further? When you read that you realise that makes no sense and yet how many times have you 'followed-up' with someone after a networking event? Once you get back from a networking event spend some time filing and sorting business cards you have received.

Email Follow-up: Email anyone whose card you have; say 'hi, nice to meet you, you can follow me on Facebook' or look them up on social media. In terms of timing, 24 hours later is perfect, when you are likely to still be fresh in their mind. Follow-ups are the easiest way to solidify any developing relationships. I usually direct them to join my mailing list or maybe join theirs. That way you still keep up, connect and engage with their business, without the hassle of piles of business cards. Sales models of networking suggest there needs to be seven positive exposures, on average, before individuals will buy from you.

Deliver: If you say you are going to do something either via follow-up or during an event, then make sure you, well, do it. This helps to strengthen and deepen relationships but not delivering makes you look unreliable, which in turn gives you and your small business a bad vibe.

Your blog and social media platforms such as Facebook and Twitter keep you in 'light' contact with people you have met. It's one of your soft follow-ups that you can engage in without pushing any sales patter at people. I usually head straight to social media and follow them on my favourite platforms (Facebook and Twitter) but you will find that most small business owners will head to LinkedIn.

However, if like me you prefer Facebook and Twitter look at how you can engage on these platforms after meeting someone at a networking event. If you like using Twitter lists then consider adding people to your relevant list. Follow them on Facebook and join local networking Facebook groups. By following up and using social media this strengthens developing relationships by keeping channels of communication open. You no longer have to be a stranger once an event has ended as social media enables you to keep the conversations going, literally in some cases before you have even left the event. Relationships are formed online which is probably why the art of follow-up has been lost slightly as we regard this online interaction as follow-up. Social media, especially the rise of closed Small Business Facebook Groups acting like safe havens/forums online, enables us to build and develop upon those networking connections making them stronger and more credible. Most events supply lists of people attending, alongside any hashtags being used on social media. This makes it really easy for individuals to find out what other businesses are attending, a bit about them and what they do. Social media is a super easy way to introduce yourself enabling you to start conversations and break the ice (and you know hide behind the computer).

What do you think makes face to face networking successful? Word of mouth; I want people to recommend me to their friends. The majority of my customers, readers and clients have come through people I have met networking, whether they themselves use my services or not. We buy from people we like, connect with or have built a relationship with. Being likeable is your networking superpower. Just think, how many times have you seen the investors on Dragon's Den part with huge amounts of cash purely upon the basis that they like someone, not necessarily their business idea at that time, but they can see themselves working with that person. It happens in most episodes.

"Always deliver more than expected."

Larry Page, founder of Google.

When I give small talks on blogging, I always suggest people tag me in their tweets, when promoting their blog posts and I'll retweet to my following. I always go and read their posts too and offer advice, suggestions or leave a comment, no-one is expecting it but it not only solidifies my standing as an expert in blogging (in their eyes) but it shows them I'm a nice person, I'm interested in helping them and their business.

Networking is vital for small businesses, it's a relatively cost effective and fun way to promote yourself. And, in this technical world, it exists in different flavours and for all kinds of people – even the shy!

ONLINE NETWORKING

"So much social media and we're more isolated than ever before"

Ruby Wax, How To Be Human: The Manual.

Technology has opened many doors and even carved new careers and business ideas that 10 years ago wouldn't have been possible. Take companies like Uber, People Per Hour or Deliveroo. These small businesses do not hold stock or even really employ individuals. In 2017 it was reported that around 5 million people in the UK are employed in this type of way, known as a "gig economy" (BBC News 'What is the gig economy?'). Whilst the freelancer has complete flexibility and control over how much they work, enabling them to prioritise other aspects of their life (like children), employers only pay for work done and don't incur staff costs, sickness pay, holiday pay or minimum wages. Proving a bit of a win-win for everyone.

What else can technology do for small businesses? Technology enables the 'gig economy' and time-poor freelancers such as parents, to run a business from virtually anywhere, soft play, in the car, at the park – all at the touch of a button, making the work-life balance slightly easier. However, our reliance on technology can have a negative impact on the way small business owners' network and build strong, long lasting connections. Some days, you don't actually speak to another real-life person. Yes, you might have pitched to some major players or scored a massive order, but you never actually spoke to anyone and soon email becomes your go-to method of communication. We forget how to read body language, communicate verbally and in a sense make friends. Face to face networking is a really useful tool for maintaining and developing your interpersonal skills.

When I first started Charlie Moo's, I felt intimidated, inexperienced and that I had nothing to offer which stopped me attending face-to-face networking events. Instead, I hid behind my computer screen and networked online. I used social media to increase my small business knowledge and develop confidence as a small business owner. Social media is great for developing stories and providing a human/real life side to your small business; remember people buy from people they know and like. Online networking enables you to connect with your core audience. Sharing your personality and expertise, provides you with an accessible platform to become that "go to" person in your industry.

Building your brand online can make it easier to take these skills offline. As with networking face-to-face, online networking is still about building relationships rather than selling to specific individuals. Look at how you present yourself, don't link dump to your website and then go away; always read what others are asking, engage, offer advice, support, hints and tips. Start conversations or join in with them – this is the key to successful networking on and offline. Use social media to keep conversations and interactions going or to get immediate responses to questions.

If you are a business which struggles to find the time for regular face-to-face networking, or haven't found one that suits your needs then I recommend Twitter, Facebook and LinkedIn with the best online resources to begin building quality small business relationships.

TWITTER

Is an excellent resource, particularly for interacting and engaging with small businesses through designated hours i.e. Dorset Hour (#DorsetHour Monday nights 7:30pm-8:30pm) or #elevenseshour Monday to Friday 11am. Twitter is a great way to network with other businesses and get to know people from the safety of your own space.

Top Twitter Tips: Follow the right people. Again, it's not a vanity numbers thing (although yes that is nice) there's no etiquette that suggests you must follow everyone who follows you.

Be PR savvy. Twitter is awesome for increasing your PR profile. Follow magazines, websites, journalists and newspapers relevant to your small business.

Engagement: There is a clear correlation between engagement and follower growth, website traffic and sales. Interact with your followers and the people you follow, take an interest in what they're doing. Whilst I appreciate this can be time consuming, commit to utilising a hashtag hour each day. I have found concentrated interaction like that has led to an increase in followers/drives traffic to my website and also provides me with a moment of socialisation and networking.

FACEBOOK

Of course, every small business worth its salt has a Facebook Small Business Page with varying degrees of success. Some small businesses I know only sell via their Facebook Page others struggle to engage their core audience at all, but with any networking you have to be consistent. You need to update it every day and interact with your customers/clients/audience. I tend to schedule a month's worth of content in advance as I just don't know when something may crop up that means I don't post live. Ideally you should be using the formula 4-1-1.

- 4 posts about support and advice as this helps to build trust.
- 1 product/direct link post.
- 1 human contact based post.

Think about your language, using simple, non-industry wording will make it much easier for your followers to engage and make real conversations with you. You can easily get sucked into a Facebook black hole so give yourself time limits and set alarms when it's time to stop. I tend to work in short blocks of 15 minutes, two or three times a day.

Recently there has also been a huge boom in specialist and subject-specific Facebook groups. These are fantastic forums for connecting with others in your niche, promoting your small business and building your network tribe. Facebook groups provide a way to connect with others in your small business genre, sometimes worldwide. This is great for growth and development. Social networking, we can easily get so caught up in the media aspect of sharing content, that we forget about the social side of it. The great thing about Facebook groups is that moderators can set the privacy levels. Lemur Linkup for example is completely private, anything that has been posted can only be seen by those within the group, making it a safe haven to ask questions.

LinkedIn

What is LinkedIn and should you be using it? I'm not a massive fan of LinkedIn myself I prefer Facebook and Twitter for connecting with other business owners, but LinkedIn is utilised by professionals because "LinkedIn is a business and employment-oriented service." (Wikipedia 2018). There are a few top things to include when creating your LinkedIn Profile, or if you have one it's a good opportunity to go back and edit it to enhance how effectively you utilise it from now on.

Use Your Real Name: Unlike other platforms, you have to be a proper grown up on LinkedIn, no room for CharlieMoos or Mummyof3 here, only Joanne Dewberry will do. LinkedIn is a 'professional' platform connecting business leaders, influencers, employers posting jobs and job seekers posting their CVs.

Use a Professional Image: Clear background, no children, pets or wine! (sorry)

Customise the URL: Like all social media platforms, utilising the URL facility enables you to share directly on business cards and email signatures. Some corporate brands will ask on a job application to view your LinkedIn profile. It makes it easier across the board for people to find you too.

Your LinkedIn Profile is NOT Your CV: Make it natural, share your skills and expertise but remember the key to LinkedIn is making connections so although you should boast your skills don't try and oversell.

Skills: You can add a vast number of skills to your LinkedIn profile however it's important to be endorsed in the areas you want to be an expert in so for me that would be blogging, social media, online networking and small business. Adding skills encourages other LinkedIn users to endorse you in these areas, in turn you will rank higher in searches for specific skills. LinkedIn actively encourages you to add a minimum of five. Don't forget to endorse other small business owners' skills too.

Recommendations and Endorsements: Ask former clients or employers to leave recommendations or mini reviews of your skills and work completed.

Build Your Connections: LinkedIn is all about networking so network. Build credible links and connections. You can do this by importing your email contact list or checking out those people associated with the same schools and colleges as you. Obviously after a few networking sessions you have a glut of business cards to trawl through as well.

Be Seen as an Expert: LinkedIn has a blog platform too called Pulse. Every so often write a piece that demonstrates your expertise and skill set, knowledge and post direct onto your LinkedIn Profile rather than just sharing from your regular blog. You can also repurpose your popular content from your blog too, this is a great way to widen your audience and target new readers.

Make Your LinkedIn Profile Engaging: Add examples of work, presentations, photos, graphics, slideshows, videos to create engaging media rich content.

Remember to be yourself: Be authentic. Be real. Connections are forged through people not businesses. Person first, business second. The way in which you behave on social media should reflect your brand and ethos, and also how you are naturally. Building connections face-to-face will make you far more memorable than a successful social media campaign.

CHAPTER SEVEN

NETWORKING LABELS; WHO ARE YOU?

yth: You have to be an aggressive player in small business to come out on top.

Fact: Networking is an innovative way to promote yourself and business without having to sell. Building better connections between your communities only strengthens your network aiding your business twofold. During my research not only through numerous networking events but also reading others take on networking, I came across an abundance of labels, types of people you'll come across at networking events and our styles of networking. It probably won't surprise you but even the way in which you network has labelled connotations assigned to it. Yes, that's right, why do we like to give everything a label? Give and Take (Adam Grant) puts people into three categories; givers, takers and matchers.

Givers: Givers are those people who inject energy and a sense of helpfulness into the group, this in turn opens up better more authentic business opportunities and relationships. They give without any strings attached, as givers are not looking for anything tangible in return other than a genuine expression of thanks. When I read Give and Take, I knew straight away I was a giver, but wondered if this

120

could be my downfall? Do I give far more than I take? Should we be (or I) be more balanced in our networking approach? Do I even remember to take at all? Then Grainne Reynolds (Times to Treasure) said.

"You, Joanne, are a networking giver. Always encouraging and so generous in sharing info and advice, amongst other things. You have made me aware of business awards and encouraged me to enter, I even won! This would never have happened without you. Also, you have advised on lots of other social media business stuff too not to mention the self-employed networking socials. So much energy, generosity and support!"

This made me realise I'm happy with being a networking giver. I have provided and enabled many small businesses to grow, develop, win awards and collaborate with others. As a small business owner, I am revered, admired and respected for that and at the forefront of other small business owners' minds in a good way. I'm always thanked and I lose track of the number of gifts, flowers and wine I have received which means the world to me. If we think back to happiness, being happy, sharing and making others happy provided me with more emotional than financial compensation, I strive on the feel-good factor. I'm motivated by contributing, connecting people and sharing knowledge with others for nothing but a feeling, I never expect anything in return. And I'm OK with that, actually I love it!

What can you offer? Rather than going in with what can they offer you? This shift in mindset increases the feel-good factor, boosts your self-confidence and makes you an excellent and fulfilled giver. Reap what you sow.

Takers: Takers will always attempt to balance any networking relationships in their favour by taking far more than they will give in return. We've all come across these kinds of people before, self-servers only interested in furthering their own path. They do not see the benefit of working with others, or developing meaningful relationships, they are just looking for a quick fix.

When developing networking relationships always look to create win-win situations, whereby both parties feel they have got the best deal from the relationship. Think back to a time where you have worked with an individual and felt like the relationship was one sided; where you left feeling like you didn't get a lot from it but worked really hard for the other person. Or maybe you have a small business acquaintance who is always asking for help, support, referrals but provides nothing in return. These kinds of relationships are toxic and draining, not only time wise but mentally as well.

However, through my research on networking relationships I realised it's important to find out why someone is being a taker, before assuming this relationship is toxic (although in the majority of cases it is). Claire Addiscott, Addiscott Pet Foods, "*I think I am a taker, your first year of business is tough and I had so little knowledge about what I was embarking on as it was a completely new direction for me. I had so much learning to do! I have taken every free course I can find, joined free networking groups, asked people questions and sought free advice! I try to give back where I can but my inexperience means my knowledge is often not as broad as others. One day I hope the balance will flip and I'll be the giver and help other 'newbies' through the same experience."*

Matchers: This is the most common group of individuals at networking events, as it works upon the principle of giver and taker, instilling a degree of equal balance. You take from me I take from you, give to me I give to you, creating a feeling of fairness. However, the individual is always thinking about themselves and their needs (or the needs of their current clients/skill set) foremost. The idea of matchers fits the BNI Philosophy (a paid subscription networking group) perfectly *"if I give you business, you'll want to give me business."* Really most of the people you meet at networking events will be a matcher. Whilst this works in some situations it might mean that you don't take into consideration the wider networking picture, developing a tribe, building relationships and making friends.

But wait; I found a lot more networking labels, I kid you not! If you don't feel like you connected with any of Adam Grant's ideas you might like one of these…

Protectors: A protector aims to stay safe, no matter what. These individuals are wary of both takers and givers, because they can't distinguish between the two. Protectors feel like all networking interactions carry the risk of being taken advantage of, causing them to neither give nor take and become one of life's lurkers by remaining safe holding back and keeping their distance.

Be a Connecter: Unless you are very confident and self-assertive, that first moment entering a new group (or any group; I still get butterflies going to Lemur Linkup) is daunting. If you aren't going with a business colleague or friend make yourself known to the hosts. Networking group hosts are brilliant connectors; they make themselves known to everyone making them the perfect ally to introduce you to others. Connectors want to help others to succeed and grow via their networking opportunities and from this other collaborations and business will often follow. A connector works by actively listening to gather information about each person; they are action-oriented working towards connecting as many people as they can.

Networking Karma: This sits nicely alongside the idea of being a giver in my mind. Networking karma looks at placing emphasis on what you put in. It's clear in my eyes that what you give to networking is what you will receive in return. If you turn up and are only interested in handing out all your business cards in one fell swoop you are unlikely to make a good impression and get anything in return other than an impersonal business card. The more small business owners you connect with, the more who will connect with you. When you start to understand and build relationships with others this will naturally lead to you seeing connections for your friends, who are then likely to return the favour and provide you with introductions. This way of networking develops organically, doing things without looking for instant gratification, as the saying goes 'what goes around comes around' or let's just chuck in another cliché 'treat people the way you wish to be treated'.

When looking at karma it's a good opportunity to talk about the principle of Law of Attraction (LOA) Example: if you say 'please don't rain, please don't rain' then you are focusing on rain and therefore attracting it to you as per the law of attraction. So instead change it to 'it's lovely and sunny/warm/dry'. For me, sometimes it's nice to pass opportunities on or help others because I want to, not for anything specific in return. However, The Law of Attraction states that what we put out we will receive in return. If we are always thinking negative thoughts then negative things will happen. Networking is the same.

Getting To Know You: You can never expect to do business with people you don't know or trust and likewise people won't want to work with you if they don't know you. I'm all about the clichés but it's true; you buy from people you like, trust and respect. This can be your networking superpower, simply just being nice (it's incredibly underrated!), someone that people like, especially if your small business is one in a saturated industry. The beauty of networking is that you connect with new people, and then you are able to connect other people to people. Almost like a real-life LinkedIn platform, whereby your connections are 1st generation, 2nd generation and 3rd generation. If we look at the theory of Six Degrees of Separation, originally set out by Frigyes Karinthy (1929) suggests that all living things and everything else in the world are six or fewer steps away from each other. We are therefore able to connect two people via a chain of 'a friend of a friend' statements in a maximum of six steps. Meaning any connections, we make via networking both online and offline will eventually lead us to the "mother" of all connections in six people or less. Even that mum at the school gate who asked you "what do you do?" can ultimately lead somewhere special. You just never know.

Talk about your business but also ensure you listen to what they have to say in return, with literally every single person you meet. If you talk to five people about your business and they then share this with five of their friends, who then talk to five friends, well then, the world is your oyster, it's that snowball effect. Then before you know it just via word of mouth, lots of people know who you are, but more importantly are actively talking about you and your business. I should mention here this is true for both good and bad comments about your business. Again, the way you make people feel will impact what they say. This is another reason to be approachable and someone other businesses like, respect and want to work with. Respect and understand the differences in people, their core values, business ethos and simply the way they conduct themselves. These differences might be just what you need in the future.

Never underestimate the power of local networking as your support network. Even if you are a global business or selling online, having real life people around you is vital.

"I think if you can find local support it can really help especially as working from home can get quite lonely."

Emma Reed, author.

"I joined the Athena before moving to Bournemouth from Surrey last year. Three people at the inaugural meeting stayed in contact with me while I remained there until I moved and gave advice and offered help. I didn't know anyone in Bournemouth so having this support gave me so much positivity around the move as I was leaving good friends but I knew there were nice people waiting for me here! I'd class them all as new friends now. And, networking groups like Lemur seem to offer that too – that friendliness, help and support – really invaluable for anyone, but definitely for a relocator like me!" Lou Devine, The PR Suite

Friendliness shouldn't be underestimated, sometimes you will go to a networking event and even know people there but if the atmosphere isn't relaxed and you don't feel comfortable you won't make those connections regardless of how amazing they might be for your business.

CHAPTER EIGHT

NETWORKING GOALS

I f there's one thing that successful small businesses have in common, it is a strong professional network. Remember; YOU is often far more important than any service or product you will ever sell, people buy from people. Whilst this is a key factor in networking it can still be beneficial to you and your small business to set some networking goals.

Prioritise Networking and Accountability

- **Prioritise Networking**: Without scheduling or diarising time to actively seek out an event to attend, networking just won't happen. Make networking a part of your marketing plan, giving networking a value within your business rather than as an afterthought. I set myself 2-3 hours per week purely to network which is usually one event per week. It's a minimal impact on my working hours but maximum effect on my productivity.

- **Accountability**: Networking makes you accountable. How many times during a conversation have you said you want to do something or you want something specific to happen within your small business? The act of saying those words out loud to others, makes you accountable. Think how you would feel when you next meet and you haven't achieved or even thought about it again?

What does being accountable mean?

Accountable; Adjective

- Subject to the obligation to report, explain, or justify something; responsible; answerable.
- Capable of being explained; explicable; explainable.

Accountability can mean different things in different situations. For example, an auditor will see accountability as numerical/financial, *"legal professionals as a constitutional arrangement; and philosophers as an ethical issue."* (Ngoasong, Creating Futures: Sustainable Enterprise and Innovation, 2017) being accountable to me means that my external (my accountability group/networking support) and internal (me, my business, what I want to achieve) obligations work together in order to get things done and achieve my small business goals.

We are people pleasers and find it far harder to disappoint another person than we do to disappoint ourselves, therefore having an accountability partner or group means you are far more likely to hit your goals/targets.

According to the American Society of Training and Development, individuals are 65% more likely to meet a goal once committing it to another person. The chances of success increase to 95% when these individuals build in ongoing meetings with their accountability group or partner to check in on their progress. An accountability group or partner makes you more likely to succeed not only providing motivation and pressure to complete goals but they are often able to offer tools and resources to help further each other's ventures:

> *"I know that if I hadn't plucked up the courage to join a small goal setting accountability group, which is very out of my comfort zone, I'd never have written any goals and therefore would never have achieved any."*
>
> *Trisha Reece, Virtual PA Services*

Once we commit to another human being, we get things done. Fear of disappointment or ridicule (which I think I can hand on heart say my accountability group would never do) stops us from sitting on our laurels.

Writing down your intentions: The act of writing your intentions, goals and dreams down alters the way you see them as you use a completely different part of the brain to process information when it's written down. Writing down your intentions also makes them REAL. Write them down, put them in your diary, on your wall anywhere where you will be visually motivated.

COLLABORATIONS

"Collaborate with people you can learn from."

Pharrell Williams

Why are collaborations important?
#collaborationovercompetition

"Sarah, Biscuits by Sarah B, and I met at a local women in business networking group and as a direct result we started working together to develop a schedule of preschool classes and summer holiday workshops. Collaborating together not only increases exposure and brand awareness for both of our businesses. But by working together we are halving the workload of our events and able to reach more clients. Individually it would be tricky to run a preschool session for such a large group, but together we can manage a variety of activities whilst keeping both the children and parents happy." Alexia Browning, Made By Me Craft Parties

COLLABORATIONS HELP YOUR SMALL BUSINESS TOO

Grow Your Audience: When I collaborate with a brand or small business, they usually share the content with their audience in turn providing me with exposure to a whole new set of people. When any small business owner attends one of my events, they always tag me in social media meaning I reach a number of individuals I haven't before without even trying. Hopefully they will read more of my content, attend my events or buy my products/services and maybe want to work with me themselves in the future. The brands themselves will also be exposed to my audience, the one I have curated, cultivated and grown, they may not even have heard of this brand previously.

Become an Expert in Your Genre: You want to use every opportunity you possibly can or have to position yourself as an expert in your given small business genre/industry and collaborating with others is a perfect way to cement this.

Build A Team: There is no I in TEAM. Building a network/support/tribe around you will not only make you stronger as a person but also provide depth and sustainability to your small business. Collaborations produce innovation and to some extent develop creativity. Some of the best ideas and projects I've worked on have been through collaborations. For example, even the simple task of brainstorming is 100% better when there are others involved, people need people to feed off each other's ideas and push our creative boundaries further.

CONCLUSION AND REFERENCES

We have discussed what successful networking doesn't look like: turning up once and handing out a shed load of business cards. Successful networking is all about building and developing relationships. Relationships that continue after meetings have ended via social media or collaborations. Relationships built on mutual trust, respect and friendship. Treat other small business owners how you wish to be treated. Use your networking group to your advantage by always asking for referrals, endorsements and recommendations online. But do this in return too.

Focus on a few groups both online and offline, get to know these people really well and build your support network/tribe. This will make your connections stronger than trying to go to every networking group possible where you will become overwhelmed and a diluted presence.

If formal or traditional groups don't work for you consider trying something different. You might want to consider less conventional networking opportunities. Back in the day with Networking Mummies UK Ltd we used to run Speed Networking Events which are a great way for you to meet new businesses that you wouldn't normally work with or probably even speak to. Just sometimes the most unusual alliances and collaborations work the best! Speed networking is

138

based on the idea of speed dating, three minutes each to tell each other about your business then ding-ding move on to the next person. Or Netwalking, co-working and fun activities like my Self-employed Team Building Socials all provide opportunities to network and build relationships.

Working from home can be a lonely experience, and social networking is great, but, for me, there's nothing like a bit of personal interaction to get your creative juices flowing and your motivation sky high. If there are no local small business networking groups or you haven't found one that is a good fit for you and your business, you can be sure there are other small business owners thinking exactly the same thing. The solution is simple: start your own. You'll be surprised by how many groups are started in this manner. I guarantee if you check out every 'About Us' page for a networking group it will start along the lines of; "I enjoyed the support and motivation I got from networking groups and I looked for one that I could take my children along to, as childcare for two was going to be difficult. But there weren't any groups like that! So, I decided to create it myself..." Michelle Childs Founder of BizMums.

KEY POINTS

- Keywords to think about when networking, grow, know, like, trust.
- Networking is a great way to remind people you exist.
- Meeting others with skill sets you can recommend to others or maybe use yourself.
- Build rapport.

- Small opportunities are often the beginning of great enterprises.
- Nurturing small business growth.
- Philosophy of giving back.

You are now armed with the information you need to get out there and network. The next step is execution. Get out there and do it.

NETWORKING 101: (this analogy is taken from a Facebook meme no original source)

So many of you watched 'Bird Box' because you saw someone post about it on social media or your friends and family talked to you about it. (A record-breaking debut for Netflix!!) Or at LEAST you know what it is, and you can make a decision on whether you will watch it or not by your family or friends' feedback.

Well this, my friend, this is what networking looks like.
The future of business!
Netflix did not have to spend a PENNY on their marketing.
YOU ALL DID IT FOR THEM.... For FREE!!
Do you see how that works?

So next time you scroll past your friend working their side hustle, (or main hustle for some of us) don't be too quick to judge or ignore... and remember, a simple like, comment, or share GREATLY helps their business and is so very much appreciated.

If you can help Netflix line their corporate pockets, surely you can help someone you know make their business work and dreams come true!?

UK Networking Groups

Nationwide Groups

Athena Network
BizMums
Business Biscotti
Business Buzz
The Family Network Ltd
Ladies Who Latte
UK Jelly
Fabulous Networking
Single Mums Business Network
Drive The Partnership Network
4N
WiRE Women in Rural Enterprise.
Mums In Business Association
Network My Club
NatWest Boost
WIBN (Women in Business Network)
Network of Women
FSB
The Business Network

North West England:

m62connections
Colony Networking
Unique Ladies Chorley

North East England

Durham Business Club
Morpeth Women's Network

Yorkshire & Humberside

Perfect People
Simply Networking
Yorkshire Network

South East England

Real Networking
Mum Plus Entrepreneur: Crawley
The Mumpreneur Networking Club
Collabor8
Cornerstones Networking
Fursty Foresters Society
Hampshire Supper & Curry Club
The ONLE Network
The Ribbons Network
Petworking
How Does She Do It
Dorking Mums In Business
Heavenly Network
She Means Business: Dorking
Working Mums Go Wild Walk: Dorking
Affinity Business Initiative: Hastings
Enterprise Connextions

East of England

POP Connect
Cambridge Social Meetup
The Marketing Meetup Cambridge
Business Owners' Open Mastermind
Riverport Business Club - St Ives and St Neots
Optimisey – SEO Meetup

Scotland

Edinburgh Mumpreneur
Edinburgh EGG,
Business Gateway Edinburgh City Council
Edinburgh University Business School
Midlothian Ladies Club,
Scottish Business Mums

Wales

Introbiz UK Ltd
Uno Networking
Bridging Wales
Network She

Northern Ireland

Mums at Work (MAW)
Friday Night Mashup

West Midlands:

The Connexion for Women in Business
Nurture Network: Lichfield

East Midlands

TDPN Showcases
Love Ladies Business Group
The Connexion for Women in Business
The Melton Rotary Enterprise Group
Genuine Connections

South West England:

Tamar Business Network
BoostTorbay
Exeter Business Club
Chudleigh G12 Business Networking
South Devon Business Club
Professionelle – Business Networking for Women
Devon Business Alliance
Fempower Women's Network
Mindful Business Netwalking
The Exeter HR Network
Cloud, Collaboration & Coffee
The Samphire Club Friday Lunch
Bizzy Networking
Lemur Linkup
DWiB (Dynamic Women in Business)
Poole Business Owners Community
Pure Networking
Bridport Networking Group
You Are The Media
The ONLE Network
Wimborne Women in Business
Lake Yard Business Club
Local Business Rocks
Word Gets Around Networking: Taunton
Women Mean Biz: Bristol
We Mean Biz: Bristol

London

West End VA Meetup (Charing Cross)
Sharing Social London
The Mumpreneur Networking Club
Ealing Business Buddies
E4 Women in Business
POP Connect

This list is not exhaustive.   Try FindNetworkingEvents.com

REFERENCES

- Achor, Shawn. The Happiness Advantage, The Seven Principles That Fuel Success and Performance at Work, Ebury Publishing (2010)
- BBC News. What is the gig economy? Available at https://www.bbc.co.uk/news/business-38930048 (2017)
- BBC News. Crossing Divides. Available at https://www.bbc.co.uk/news/uk-47369648 (2019)
- Celeste, Jill. The Key To Authentic Networking Available at http://www.jillceleste.com/key-authentic-networking/ (2017)
- Consumer Insights team of Microsoft Canada. Attention Spans. Available at https://www.prc.za.com/2016/11/18/attention-spans-report-microsoft-2015/ (2015)
- DeNuchi, Patti. Networking and Happiness. Available at https://intentionalnetworker.com/2014/06/networking-happiness/ (2014)
- Grant, Adam. Give or Take: Why Helping Others Drives Our Success. W&N (2014)
- Independent Professionals and Self Employed (ISPE). Exploring the rise of self-employment in the modern economy. Available at https://www.ipse.co.uk/resource/exploring-the-rise-of-self-employment-in-the-modern-economy-pdf.html (2008.)
- Karinthy, Frigyes. Chains (Láncszemek) (1929)
- Mehrabian, Albert. The 7-38-55% communication rule. Available at https://www.bl.uk/people/albert-mehrabian (1967)
- Montoya, Inigo. The Princess Bride Film (1987), motion picture, 20th Century Fox, USA

- Ngoasong, Michael. Sacchetti, Silvia. Creating Futures: Sustainable Enterprise and Innovation, The Open University, (2017)
- Payton, Susan. The Business of Mums. Available at https://www.britmums.com/mums-in-business-round-up-networking-tips/ (2016)
- Regus The Workplace Revolution. Available at https://www.regus.co.uk/work-uk/wp-content/uploads/sites/131/2017/04/Report3.pdf (2017)
- Robbins, Tony Inspirational Quotes. Available at https://www.tonyrobbins.com/tony-robbins-quotes/ (2020)
- Rubin, Gretchen. The Happiness Project, HarperPaperbacks, (2009)
- Tobin, Michael. Live Love Work Prosper, Third Millennium, (2018)
- Wax, Ruby. How To Be Human: The Manual, Penguin Life, (2018)

QUOTES

Alexia Browning, Made By Me Craft Parties

Albert Einstein

Amanda Davey, Tilia Publishing UK

Amanda Johnson, Virtual Assistant Coaching and Training

Anne Cornish, Anne Cornish VA

Angel Alzona, Art Room Collective.

Claire Addiscott, Addiscott Pet Foods,

Emma Reed

Darren Blackstock, PedalTalk

Franklin D. Roosevelt

Grainne Reynolds, Times to Treasure

Jackie Richmond, Lemur Landings

Jay Danzie

Jim Rohn

Jo Lee, Life Atlas Coaching

Jo Stratton, Jo's Healing Cabin

Kate Codrington

Lou Devine, The PR Suite

Larry Page, founder of Google

Mark Twain

Maya Angelou

Michelle Childs Founder of BizMums.

Natalia DaCosta, Athena Network Bournemouth

Pharrell Williams

Trisha Reece, Virtual PA Services

Other books by Joanne Dewberry

If you are a producer of handmade products, or you have a craft hobby and are thinking about taking the next step and wondering how to do it, then this book has the answers. In it you will find out:

- How to turn your hobby into a small business
- Where to sell your products, both on and offline
- How to price your products
- How to develop a unique and recognisable brand
- Where to start with visual merchandising
- How to use social media to market your business

This book not only takes you through these points in no-nonsense plain English, but has quirky craft activities to complete along the way.

Crafting A Successful Small Business
By Joanne Dewberry
Print ISBN: 978-1-90800-342-3
eBook ISBN: 978-1-90800-343-0

Printed in Great Britain
by Amazon

27935380R00086